Siobhán Rowe
11B

GCSE Music

AQA Areas of Study

- **Works seamlessly with the CGP Music Core Content book**

- **Clear and concise**

- **99.8% Elvis free**

Contents

Composition

Well, the good news is — the compositions you have to do for GCSE only need to be 2-3 minutes long. So no one's expecting you to write an opera. Something short will do it.

To Get Top Marks Include these Five Things...

1) **SOUNDS USED IN INTERESTING WAYS**
   - Once you've picked your instruments, think carefully about how they can make interesting and contrasting sounds — e.g. pizzicato bits for strings or muted bits for brass instruments.
   - Remember the limitations — e.g. clarinetists need space to breathe and beginners can often only play low notes.
   - Think about how you can use your performance space — e.g. put your performers on two different sides of a stage to give a stereo effect.

2) **BALANCED STRUCTURE**
   Organise your music with a clear, balanced structure. See Section 5 in the Core book for examples.

3) **WELL-DEVELOPED MUSICAL IDEAS**
   Don't just use a good idea once and then forget about it. Build up and develop the good bits — e.g. by changing the rhythm from short notes to long notes or the tonality from major to minor.

4) **AWARENESS OF STYLE**
   Listen to lots of music from the style you're composing in. Make your piece sound like 'the real thing' by using similar musical ideas — e.g. in a reggae song use offbeat swung quavers, syncopated bass lines and muted guitar sounds.

5) **MUSICAL TECHNIQUES AND DEVICES**
   "Techniques and devices" are those clever tricks composers have used for centuries. See P.44-45 in the Core book for loads of examples.

Decide how to Hand In Your Work

There are various ways you can hand in your completed composition...

...this isn't one of them.

WRITTEN VERSION
1) These can be in...
   - standard notation, i.e. on a stave
   - graphic notation, i.e. in symbols
   - a computer score
   - melody lines and/or lyrics and chord charts
2) Give as much information as possible. Details of dynamics, tempo, expression and articulation will all improve your mark.

RECORDING
1) You don't get any marks for recording quality but good recordings are easier to mark.
2) If you've had help from your teacher with equipment like sequencers, say so on the Candidate Record Form.
3) If your composition includes material from sources like MIDI files or samples from the Internet, that has to go on the form too.

ANNOTATION & RECORDING
1) An annotation is a description of your piece in words or diagrams.
2) If you hand in an annotation you have to hand in a recording too.

WRITTEN VERSION & RECORDING
1) You can also hand in a written version and a recording.
2) If you do this, tell the examiners which one is most like what you hoped to achieve.

Along with the composition you hand in a Candidate Record Form with details of your brief, the composing process, any help you've had from your teacher or anyone else, and any IT you've used.

I bet Beethoven never had to write a brief...

On the one hand, you've got almost two years to get these compositions sorted. On the other hand, if you don't start ASAP you might just find yourself running out of time. Best get on with it.

Coursework — Performance

The better you play, the more marks you get, so pick your pieces carefully and practise hard. Practise till your fingers bleed and the neighbours beg for mercy.

You Have to Do Two Performances

The pieces you play can be anything you like. But...

1) One of the two performances has to be a solo (though it's OK to have a simple accompaniment).
2) The other has to be an ensemble piece — anything from a duet to a full band, so long as you have an important part (playing third triangle in a full symphony orchestra won't quite cut it, I'm afraid).

So, say you play the violin — you could do a solo with piano accompaniment for one performance and a violin duet for the other.

You could play a different instrument for each performance, but it's safest to stick to what you're best at.

You Get Marks for the Quality of your Playing...

In each performance, you need to show off your 'musicality'. You get marks for —

1) *ACCURACY OF PITCH AND RHYTHM*   This bit's the easiest. Just learn the notes, play them in time and in tune. Most importantly keep going — lots of stopping and starting or slowing down for tricky bits will lose you marks. Don't worry about the odd slip because of nerves, but start off well prepared.
2) *EXPRESSION*   Your performance needs to make the audience feel something. Pay attention to stuff like dynamics, tempo, mood, articulation and phrasing. If they're not written in, work out your own.
3) *INTERPRETATION*   Use expression and playing techniques that fit the style of your piece — e.g. don't play a lullaby on a distorted electric guitar.
4) *ENSEMBLE SKILLS*   Obviously you only get marks for this when you're playing in an ensemble. Play in time with the other players. Really listen to the other parts, so you know when you should be part of the background and when you should make your part stand out. Tune up before you start and listen carefully to intonation (tuning) all the way through.

...and Marks for the Difficulty of the Piece

A really simple piece, in an easy key like C major, with easy rhythms — just crotchets and quavers — and small straightforward jumps between notes, will get one or maybe two marks for difficulty.

A piece of music in a tricky key with lots of sharps and flats, which is very fast or has complicated rhythms and difficult leaps between notes could get five or six marks for difficulty.

CHOOSE YOUR PIECES CAREFULLY

1) Ideally they should be the hardest level that you can play well.
2) If you pick something too easy, you'll be throwing away difficulty marks.
3) If you pick something too hard, you won't be able to play your best, and you'll be throwing away marks for musicality.
4) Get your music teacher or instrument teacher's advice on what to play.

Practise, Practise, Scales, Practise, Every Day, Practise...

Hmmm... How am I going to get you to take this in...
No doubt people have been going on at you about practising since you were knee-high to a piccolo...
The more my music teachers went on at me about practising, the less I felt like doing it...
       I expect you know that you need to do lots of practice. So we'll just leave it there.

The Integrated Assignment

The Integrated Assignment starts after Christmas in Year 11. You get four months to compose a piece and make a recording. Finally (and this is the cherry on the cake) you evaluate your work in a half-hour exam.

You Get a Choice of Composing Briefs to Get You Started

Before you start on the Integrated Assignment, you get a booklet of four briefs from the examiners.
There'll be one each for Areas of Study 1, 2, 4 and 5. You choose one brief to work from.
Here's a sample brief for AoS2 — Music for Dance.

You'll learn about all these things in AoS2 — make sure you use what you know in your composition.

> Compose a waltz or a polka EITHER as an accompaniment to dancing in the nineteenth century ballroom OR as a piece for performance written in the style of a dance.
> Make sure your music shows:
> - any special features of your chosen dance style
> - elements to show that you have carefully considered your chosen audience
> - a suitable structure or form
> - a variety of rhythmic and/or melodic devices to keep the tune interesting
>
> Suggested Listening:
> Chopin — *Grande Valse Brilliante* (Op.18)
> Johann Strauss the Younger — *The Blue Danube* and *Pizzicato* and *Thunder and Lightning Polkas*
> Tchaikovsky — waltz in the *Sleeping Beauty* ballet suite
> Brahms — *Liebeslieder* waltzes

You MUST stick to the brief for this composition. Don't go off at a tangent — you'll lose marks.

You can 'Realise' Your Piece in Different Ways

Once you've written your piece, you'll need to perform and record it. This is called the realisation.
There are lots of ways of tackling the realisation:

1) If you know people who play the instruments used in your piece you can do a live performance. Get plenty of rehearsals in beforehand.
2) If your piece is for instruments that aren't played by people you know, you'll have to use computer sounds in place of the real instruments.
3) You could compose a piece that uses music technology as the main 'instrument'. If you do, you'll produce your realisation on the computer as you go along.

Your realisation has to be completed in front of your teacher. You also need to hand in a score or annotation.

You Write the Evaluation under Exam Conditions

At the end of your gruelling four months of composing, you have to do a half-hour exam. This is the kind of question you'll get — all about the key points from the brief, and about what you think of the 'realisation':

- *Write about any special features that you used for your chosen dance style.*
- *How did you make your piece suitable for its intended audience?*
- *Describe the structure or form used for your piece and give a reason why you used it.*
- *What rhythmic and melodic devices did you use?*
- *What problems did you face during the realisation of your piece? How did you solve them?*
- *What bits of the final realisation worked well and why?*

Think about all the questions as you're composing and write down what you think.
Go back to your notes and refresh your memory before the exam.

25% — D'you realise that's a quarter of your marks?

The composing, realising and evaluating bits of the integrated assignment are each worth an equal number of marks. That means each one's equally important, and each one needs equal attention from you. So there.

The Listening Exam

When all the coursework's done and handed in, you can just sit back, stick a CD on and relax, can't you...
OH NO YOU CAN'T — you've got to do a listening exam. All 75 minutes of it. Whoopee-doodle-DOO.

The Listening Exam Tests All the Areas of Study

1) The Listening Exam is worth 25% of your total mark — that's a big chunk of marks.
2) As you might have guessed, it involves listening. The invigilator plays music from a CD.
   You listen to the music and answer written questions about it.
3) There are lots of bits of music to listen to. Each one has its own set of questions. You'll hear a piece
   three or four times and do all the questions for it before moving on to the next one.
4) Concentrate on answering just a few of the questions each time the music's played — it's less confusing.
5) You don't get a lot of time on this paper — think fast and write fast.
6) Each group of questions is marked with the AoS at the beginning. Check which one it is — you could
   end up listening to film music and thinking it's dance music.

Some Questions are Multiple Choice

Don't make a botch by rushing these — read all the options carefully.

 Ring the word that best describes the tonality at the end of this extract.

atonal   major   minor   pentatonic

If you get stuck — guess the answer. There's a 25% chance of getting it right.

Some Questions Just Need a Short Answer

These questions test your detailed knowledge of the AoS. They're only worth a couple of marks
so don't waste time writing your answer out in a nice long sentence — just stick it down.

Apart from the rhythm, what other elements of this
music are influenced by African music? (2 marks)

Sometimes They Give You an Outline of the Music

You could get an outline of part of the music called a 'skeleton score'. It will just show part of the music
— the melody, rhythm or lyrics, say. The skeleton score will help you with answering the question.
Often you'll be asked to fill in the pitch or rhythm of a short section of the music.

 Describe the melodic movement in bar 4.

Questions Worth Between Five and Ten Marks Need a Longer Answer

These are questions where you have to write a longer answer — either lists of words and phrases, or a
couple of paragraphs of continuous writing. To work out how much to write, look at the number of marks.

 Comment on the use of rhythm, tonality, melody, instruments
and any other features of interest you hear. (10 marks)

Shiver me timbers — 'tis the skeleton score...

If you think of an answer while the CD's playing, just use a pencil and scribble it down. The music stops
to give you writing time after each question — use that time to write the answer neatly in pen.

The Elements of Film Music

Composers use different <u>ingredients</u> to make up music. These are called <u>elements</u>.
You need to <u>know</u> how composers <u>use</u> them to create different <u>moods</u>.

Rhythm is the Pattern of Beats that you Tap your Foot to

1) <u>Rhythm</u> can be <u>fast</u> or <u>slow</u> — this is the <u>tempo</u>.
2) <u>Rhythm</u> can be <u>straight</u> (accents on the main beats) or <u>syncopated</u> (some accents on offbeats)
3) Sometimes <u>different</u> rhythms are played at the same time (these are <u>cross-rhythms</u>).
4) Rhythms can have <u>different numbers</u> of beats in a bar — this is dictated by the <u>time signature</u>.

(see core book, p6)

Melody's the Tune — the Bit you Always Remember

<u>Two</u> things are <u>important</u> when writing a <u>melody</u>:
1) The <u>set of notes</u> used to write it — that's the <u>scale</u> (see below and p14-17 of the core book).
2) The <u>shape</u> it makes — that's the <u>contour</u>. Look at this example of the <u>Star Wars</u> theme:

Notice how the <u>melody</u> is <u>shaped</u>. The <u>wide leaps</u> and <u>falling notes</u> make this theme very <u>dramatic</u>.

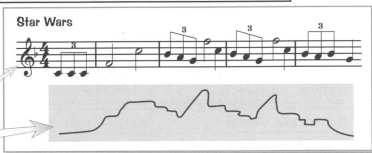

Star Wars

Tonality means the Key — it gives a Piece its Mood

1) The most <u>common</u> keys are <u>major</u> (which sounds <u>happy and bright</u>) and <u>minor</u> (which sounds quite <u>sad</u>).
2) <u>Pentatonic</u>'s a <u>five-note scale</u> — it sounds a bit <u>Chinese</u> and it's also used in <u>folk music</u>.
3) <u>Modal</u> music can sound <u>ambient</u> or <u>religious</u> (like monks singing).
4) Sometimes music has <u>no key</u> and sounds weird — this is <u>atonal</u>.
5) If <u>two tunes</u> are playing together but don't fit — this will be <u>bitonal</u>.
6) You might need to recognise different <u>chords</u> (such as <u>major</u>, <u>minor</u>, <u>diminished</u>, etc.). *(p21-26, core book)*

Texture is the Way Chords and Melody are Woven Together

1) <u>Monophonic</u> texture is when someone's playing or singing a tune on their <u>own</u>.
2) <u>Homophonic</u> (<u>harmonic</u>) texture is when the tune is <u>supported</u> by <u>chords</u>.
3) <u>Polyphonic</u> (<u>contrapuntal</u>) texture is when different lines <u>weave</u> in and out of each other.

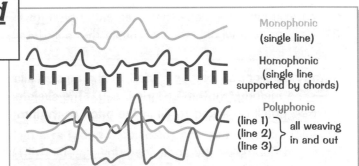

Monophonic (single line)

Homophonic (single line supported by chords)

Polyphonic
(line 1)
(line 2)   all weaving
(line 3)   in and out

Dynamics are all about How Loud Things are

1) Music can be <u>quiet</u> (*piano, p*) or <u>loud</u> (*forte, f*).
2) It might <u>suddenly</u> go from <u>quiet to loud</u> — <u>terraced dynamics</u>.
3) It might <u>gradually</u> get <u>louder</u> (crescendo) or <u>gradually</u> get <u>quieter</u> (diminuendo).
4) <u>Silence</u> is important too. Think about it. When everything's <u>quiet</u> it can really <u>freak</u> you out. *(see p11, core book)*

You Need to Pick Out Different Instruments

1) <u>Learn</u> the different <u>sections</u> of the <u>orchestra</u> and <u>instruments</u> that make up <u>bands</u>.
2) Do plenty of <u>listening</u> so you know what they <u>sound</u> like. (See Section 7 of the core book.)

Devices Used in Film

Composers who write film music use similar techniques.
You'll be able to steal these ideas when composing your own music.

Using Music to Show a Certain Time or Place is Common

1) Music in films tells us when and where the action is set.
2) If the film is set in India, the composer will probably use some Indian music.
3) If the film is set in America, the American national anthem might be played. It's not exactly rocket science.
4) A film set in the 1960s might include chart music (pop songs) from the sixties.

Look Out for the Leitmotif in Most Film Music

1) The leitmotif is the main tune in the film.
2) It represents a particular object, idea or character in the story and often returns in the background or in an altered form.
3) Here is the leitmotif from the Indiana Jones films. (Note — it pops up every time Indiana is about to do something heroic.)

Indiana Jones

You can Create a Sense of Urgency Using Repeated Ideas

This can be done in three ways:
1) Ostinato is a musical pattern that's repeated while the rest of the music changes around it. In pop music it's called a riff.
2) When the main theme is repeated in the bass, it's called a ground bass.
3) Notes that keep repeating while the rest of the music moves on are called pedal notes. If one note is held on, it's called a drone.

Using Imitation can Give the Feeling of a Chase

1) Imitation is when one part copies another.
2) An example of a piece that uses imitation a lot is a fugue.
3) A canon is a whole piece of music that's imitated. It's sometimes called a round.

Repetition helps to Link Different Bits of a Film

1) Repetition is when a section of music is played again.
2) Repetition of a phrase (p28, core book) at a higher or lower pitch is called a sequence.
3) Repetition helps the audience bring together different bits of a film. Repetition helps the audience...

Music should be Structured and Timed to Fit the Film

1) Film directors need music to be synchronised with the action to the split second.
2) The different sections of a film show different moods, e.g. from fighting to romance. The music can easily be chopped up and moved around using samplers and computer programs like Cubase and Pro-Tools.

There are Lots of Famous Songs in Films

1) A song can be used as the title track but can return in the background later — like a leitmotif (e.g. the song 'Everything I do (I do it for you)' pops up many times in the film 'Robin Hood Prince of Thieves').
2) Most film music is meant for just the audience to hear, but sometimes the director wants the characters to hear the music as well — this is called diegetic music. A good example of this is that bit in The Bodyguard when they're dancing in the bar to that horrible song that really really annoys me.

The Western

Ahhh... westerns — cowboys and Indians, saloon bars, honky-tonk pianos and crooked sheriffs.
Men in funny hats fighting other men with different funny hats. And that wonderfully distinctive music...

Traditional Instruments give you a feel for Time and Place

1) Westerns are set in 19th century North America. They generally tell a simple story
about good against evil, and they can often be very dramatic and violent.

2) In some westerns, composers use music from the time to set the scene.
E.g. guitarist Ry Cooder composed music for The Long Riders (1980).
He used traditional music and instruments:

jew's harp

percussion

side or Spanish guitar, banjo, fiddle, mandolin, honky-tonk piano

tin flute, harmonica

trumpet, trombone and horns

3) Melody and harmony are simple (like the bad guy) but catchy with lots of bendy notes.

The Music can Create a Range of Moods

1) There's often a load of people playing at once, creating a polyphonic texture
(more than one line at once). This can give a feeling of a buzzing community.

2) Most music for westerns is in major keys but changes to minor or becomes
dissonant (unpleasant on the ear) when something goes wrong in the story.

3) Westerns are full of action (e.g. gunfights) so the tempo and dynamics change to fit the drama.
E.g. when building to a climax in a fight sequence, the music might get louder and faster.

4) Or like in The Long Riders in the last gunfight, silence is used to build tension.
(You can hear breathing and bullets flying through the air.)

Sometimes Characters in the Film can Hear the Music

1) Traditional folk songs are used in westerns and can be sung or played by characters
on screen. (Diegetic music — see p8.) E.g. when Jessie James gets married
in The Long Riders there's a band playing and everyone's dancing.

2) This helps to give you a feel for the simple traditional community that the film is set in.

Western Soundtracks Don't Just use Traditional Music

1) John Barry's Dances With Wolves (1990) soundtrack is orchestral. You almost never hear orchestras
in westerns, but in this case it was used deliberately to create more mood and emotion than in most
westerns. It's a more realistic storyline than many westerns (such as The Long Riders), and shows
lots of pain and sadness. The main character (John Dunbar, played by my least favourite actor
Kevin Costner) has his own theme, which appears throughout Dances With Wolves as the leitmotif
(main tune). It returns in different forms and is imitated in different sections of the orchestra.
It appears whenever John Dunbar is writing his diary.

2) *And then of course there was the classic Young Guns 2: Blaze of Glory that had that Bon Jovi soundtrack.
It used some traditional western-film-style guitar sounds, but it was unmistakably 1990s soft rock.
Which made it all the more appealing to the teenage girls it was clearly aimed at...*

A friend of mine says 9:50 is 'cowboy time'...

It's because of the music. You know — ten ter ten, ten ter ten, ten ter ten ten ten.
He thinks it's clever, when in fact it's merely irritating.

Classic Horror, Science Fiction and Fantasy

Music for horror and fantasy often makes you feel like you're in <u>another world</u> or a kind of <u>nightmare reality</u>. The music can also help to <u>build tension</u> and to <u>make you jump</u>, so your <u>popcorn</u> goes everywhere.

You are Lured into a False Sense of Security

1) When music's in a calm <u>major key</u>, you don't feel like anything bad's going to happen. E.g. in <u>Jurassic Park</u> (1993), when <u>nice dinosaurs</u> walk across the hills we hear a <u>simple melody</u> in a <u>major key</u> composed by John Williams. Also, in <u>The Lord of the Rings</u> (2001-3), <u>Howard Shore</u> composed a happy piece of music to reflect the comfort and safety of the Shire.

Jurassic Park

C B   C G F C B C G F

2) <u>Beware</u> — sometimes the same <u>theme</u> comes back in an <u>altered form</u> — like in a <u>minor key</u> — to show that things have started to <u>go wrong</u>.

Tension Builds and Makes you Feel Like Something Bad is Going to Happen

1) <u>Dynamics</u> get <u>louder</u>.
2) <u>Tempo</u> gets <u>faster</u>.
3) <u>Pitch</u> gets <u>higher</u>.
4) A <u>tune</u> played earlier in a <u>scary bit</u> sometimes <u>comes back</u> to remind you.
5) Sometimes they use <u>silence</u> before a <u>loud</u> bit just to make you <u>jump</u>. Ratbags.

Composers can Keep you on the Edge of your Seat

1) <u>Snippets</u> of sound and <u>sound effects</u> are used to create a feeling of <u>unease</u> (e.g. at the beginning of Jurassic Park).
2) <u>Ostinati</u> (p8) keep the <u>audience</u> on <u>edge</u> for a long time. E.g. in <u>Halloween</u> (1978) there's an ostinato played in a <u>minor key</u> — it's then played on a <u>different note</u> to keep the audience wondering where the scary person is going next.
3) In some sci-fi films there's background music with just drums and bass, generated on <u>computers</u>, that's played under the <u>dialogue</u> throughout the film. This lets the audience know that the danger is always there.
4) <u>Sustained</u> notes create <u>suspense</u> (e.g. tremolo strings).

Unnatural Sounds can Back Up Strange Goings-On

1) <u>Unusual keys</u> and <u>time signatures</u> are used — they're not what you're expecting, so they sound odd.
2) <u>Synthesizers</u> and <u>samples</u> of bizarre <u>sounds</u> can be unnerving because you wonder what's causing them.
3) Common <u>instruments</u> or <u>voices</u> can be <u>distorted</u> using <u>computers</u>.
4) No clear <u>structure</u> is used.
5) <u>Discords</u> and <u>diminished</u> chords make it difficult to listen to.

The action can be synchronised to the music...

6) <u>Rapid scalic patterns</u> (going up and down scales) and <u>interrupted cadences</u>, <u>irregularly placed discords</u> and <u>diminished chords</u> (see Section 4, core book) can all make <u>pulse-raising</u> scenes feel more frantic.
7) In <u>Psycho</u> (1962), for every <u>stab</u> of the <u>knife</u> the <u>violins</u> also <u>stab</u> out a <u>high-pitched discord</u>. Each chord goes right through you, and makes what you're seeing on-screen feel much more real.

Just no one mention Arachnophobia — please...

Turn the TV down when you're watching a scary film and it's <u>nowhere near as nail-biting</u>. More than in any other film genre, the music in horror and fantasy is <u>crucial</u> to setting the atmosphere.

Thrillers and Spy Movies

Thrillers and spy movies are often <u>serious</u> and <u>tense</u>. There's lots of <u>action</u> and <u>dialogue</u> — so you've got to watch carefully to follow the plot. There's often <u>government involvement</u> and <u>conspiracies</u> and people dealing with <u>shadowy figures</u> and <u>underground organisations</u>. All very X-Files.

The Music Shows What's Not On-Screen

It's often the composer's job to create a <u>feeling</u> of something <u>being there</u> that's <u>not seen</u>.

1) <u>Minor</u> and more <u>dissonant chords</u> make you feel <u>uneasy</u>.
2) <u>Low pitches</u> in <u>brass</u> and <u>strings</u> sound <u>dark</u> like the <u>underground</u>.
3) <u>Percussive</u> sounds (some <u>metallic</u>) with <u>reverb effects</u> — sounds that might be heard on <u>lonely backstreets</u> — make you imagine someone <u>lurking</u> about.
4) <u>Long</u> drawn-out <u>chromatic notes</u> build <u>tension</u> — making you think <u>danger</u> is near.
5) <u>Dynamics swell</u> from <u>quiet</u> to <u>loud</u> to <u>quiet</u> as if someone's coming in and out of the <u>shadows</u>.

E.g. in <u>The Usual Suspects</u> (1995) the mystical character <u>Keyser Soze</u> is never seen, but the composer <u>John Ottman</u> had the job of <u>bringing him to life</u>. He did this by writing <u>dark</u>, <u>sinister</u> music.

Sometimes there's Lots of Layers to the Story

In <u>The Usual Suspects</u> there are various <u>devices</u> used to suggest more than one thing going on.

1) <u>Long notes</u> in the <u>foreground</u> with <u>ostinato</u> patterns in the <u>background</u>.
2) A <u>repeated pattern</u> on the <u>woodblock</u> sounds like someone's <u>on the move</u> while <u>percussive bursts</u> and <u>brass motifs</u> played on top suggest someone's trying to catch them.

Films can have their Own Theme

Everyone knows the <u>James Bond</u> theme.

1) In <u>Goldeneye</u> (1995) the <u>main theme</u> isn't heard for ages so the audience is kept in <u>suspense</u>.
2) Sometimes <u>sections of the theme</u> are heard in the <u>background</u> as a <u>reminder</u>.
3) E.g. the song <u>Goldeneye</u> was written by <u>Bono</u> and sung by <u>Tina Turner</u>. The <u>first two notes</u> of this song are the <u>same</u> as the <u>Bond theme</u> and later the <u>strings</u> also play part of the <u>main theme</u>.

The Style of Music Changes with the Mood of the Scene

1) In the <u>car chase</u> in <u>Goldeneye</u> there's an undercurrent of <u>70s funk</u> — this gives a feeling of <u>excitement without real danger</u>.
2) In the <u>casino</u>, <u>classical</u> music gives the audience the impression that Bond is somewhere <u>posh</u>.
3) In <u>St Petersburg</u> there's a <u>traditional Russian brass band</u> playing — giving a sense of <u>time and place</u>.
4) In <u>action</u> scenes, the <u>tempo and dynamics</u> build and the <u>texture</u> becomes more <u>complicated</u> — it <u>fades</u> when the <u>action stops</u> and <u>builds</u> when it <u>returns</u>.

Just no one mention Austin Powers — please...

Aaaah... good old Bond films. I reckon this is a pretty cool 'Area of Study' — just imagine the number of History students desperately wanting an excuse to sit around watching loads of tacky Bond films.

Revision Summary

It's only a short section, but you still need to check you know it all. And to be honest, it is probably the nicest bit of the syllabus — so quit your whingeing. The answers to these questions are all covered in the last few pages, so if you've learnt your stuff properly, you'll be able to answer all of them.
Do these questions until you can get them all right.

1)   What's rhythm?

2)   What's melody?

3)   What's tonality?

4)   What's texture?

5)   What are dynamics?

6)   What might a composer do with the rhythm if they're writing for a chase scene?

7)   The two most common scales are m____ and m____.

8)   What's the big difference between the moods these two scales create?

9)   In what kind of film might a composer use atonal or bitonal music?

10)   When might a diminished chord or discord be used in film music?

11)   What key might a composer use if they were writing for a funeral scene?

12)   If a trumpet is playing on its own in a funeral scene, what kind of texture would that be?

13)   Why is silence so important in film music?

14)   Give an example of a type of film (or scene) where silence might be used to create a dramatic effect.

15)   In an attack by killer rats, what would you expect to happen to the dynamics?

16)   If you had to write music for a romantic scene, what instruments might you use?

17)   How might a composer show that a film is set in, say, China?

18)   How might a composer show that a film is set in the 1950s?

19)   What's a leitmotif?

20)   Give an example of a leitmotif being used in a film you've seen.

21)   What effect might an ostinato have in a piece of film music?

22)   What is a sequence?

23)   Why is it usually dead important for the timing to be exact in film music?

24)   Give an example of a piece of diegetic music.

25)   Give three characteristics of music used in westerns.

26)   Give three characteristics of music used in horror and sci-fi films.

27)   Give three characteristics of music used in thriller and spy movies.

Dance Music — The Basics

Metre, tempo, rhythm and phrasing are the absolute basics of dance — they're the bits in the music that tell the dancers when and how to move. Here's how they work...

The Pattern of Beats is Called the Metre

The beats in a piece of music make different patterns of strong and weak beats, depending on the time signature. The pattern they make is called the metre.

Nearly all dance music has a regular metre. The strong beats make the same pattern throughout the music.

THE MAIN METRES USED IN DANCE ARE...

DUPLE METRE
2 beats per bar. It goes 'TUM tum, TUM tum'.

TRIPLE METRE
3 beats per bar. It goes 'TUM tum tum, TUM tum tum'.

QUADRUPLE METRE
4 beats per bar. It goes 'TUM tum TUM tum, TUM tum TUM tum'.

The Tempo Tells Dancers How Fast to Move

1) The movements in a dance normally fit the speed of the beat — the tempo.

2) The speed of a dance does a lot to set the mood. A pavan has a controlled tempo matching the stately movements, but a carefree Irish jig, with a lot of leaping about, has a zippier tempo.

3) Dance music that's written for listening to is often written with lots of speeding up and slowing down.

4) In dance music that's actually used for dancing the tempo stays the same all the way through a piece to make it easier for the dancers to follow the beat.

See P. 10 of the Core Content book for words to describe mood and tempo that will make the examiner purr like a tiger cub.

Dance Moves Often Follow the Rhythm

Some dances have a set rhythm that goes with set movements. E.g. in tango, the "arm out, strut across the floor and throw your partner back" move fits repeated rhythms in the music.

In formal dances the set movements often match regular phrases in the music. The phrases are usually 4 bars long. When a new phrase begins the set movements are repeated.

There are Different Types of Dance

Dads at weddings dance by jiggling from foot to foot, but there are loads of other types of dance:

1) <u>CEREMONIAL DANCE</u> — in some cultures there are traditional dances for important occasions, e.g. at Greek weddings there are special dances which all the guests join in with.

2) <u>COURT DANCE</u> — for celebrating official occasions like coronations or royal weddings.

3) <u>SOCIAL DANCE</u> — dances which take place in ballrooms/parish halls/discos/clubs.

4) <u>FOLK DANCE</u> — Morris dancing, maypole dancing and other dances performed at public events.

5) <u>DANCES THAT TELL STORIES</u> — like in classical ballet.

6) <u>INSTRUMENTAL MUSIC</u> — music that's written in the style of a dance, but meant for listening, not for actual dancing, e.g. some of the waltzes, polkas and minuets written by Chopin, Brahms and Schubert.

Show the examiners you know all the moves...

Dance is one of the Areas of Study they test in the Listening. That means you need to know all the jargon for talking about dance. You need to know it so well that it trips off your tongue quicker than a flock of ballerinas in pink satin ballet shoes, all wearing tutus, with their hair scraped into amazingly tight buns.

The Baroque Suite

The Baroque period ran from about 1600 to 1750. For AoS2 you learn about four types of Baroque dance — the <u>minuet</u>, <u>sarabande</u>, <u>gavotte</u> and <u>gigue</u>. They were often grouped together in a "<u>Suite</u>".

Baroque Suites were Rich People's Music

1) To earn a living, a composer working in Baroque times needed a patron — someone rich to pay for their music. Composers often wrote music specially for their patrons, e.g. for <u>royal events</u> or <u>church services</u> and <u>dances</u>.
2) One of the most popular types of composition for dance was the <u>suite</u>. Suites were played at <u>dances</u>, for <u>general listening</u> and to celebrate <u>big occasions</u>.
3) The most famous Baroque suites for orchestra are Bach's *Four Orchestral Suites* and Handel's *Water Music* and *Music for the Royal Fireworks*.

aaahhh...

A Suite is Made up of Contrasting Dances

A suite's made up of at least <u>four</u> contrasting dances. Composers usually <u>linked</u> them by putting them in the <u>same key</u> or the tonic minor key, e.g. D major and D minor.

These are the four you need to know:

The Minuet's an Elegant Dance

1) The minuet's in simple triple metre, usually <u>3/4</u>. It's performed at a <u>medium</u> tempo.
2) The minuet's the only Baroque dance form that was still played in the <u>Classical Period</u>. It's often used as the <u>third movement</u> of a symphony (see P.30).

The Sarabande is Slow and Serious

accent on second beat

1) A sarabande is in simple <u>triple metre</u> (3/4) just like a minuet, but it sounds very different.
2) It's <u>slower</u> and more <u>serious</u>. The <u>second beat</u> is often <u>stressed</u> heavily.
3) You'll hear lots of <u>ornaments</u> (see P.12 of the Core book) fancying up the tune. The slow beat gives the performer time to <u>fit them in</u>.

ornament

A Gavotte is Quite Quick

1) Gavottes are in simple duple metre, usually <u>2/2</u>. They go at a <u>quick</u> but stately tempo.
2) All the phrases begin with an <u>anacrusis</u> — they start halfway through the bar.
3) Gavotte tunes use <u>simple</u> rhythms and a lot of <u>sequences</u> in the melody (see P.15).

anacrusis　　　　　*sequence*

The Gigue is the Liveliest Dance

1) The gigue (say it with a French accent) is in compound duple metre, usually <u>6/8</u>.
2) This was the <u>liveliest</u> dance in the suite and usually came at the <u>end</u>.

Baroque and baroll came later...

If you get a question on Baroque suites it's <u>highly likely</u> that they'll ask you to say what type of dance is playing. Learn the stuff on this page and you'll be able to pick up some nice <u>easy marks</u>. All you have to do is work out the tempo and time signature. Once you've got that you'll know what you're listening to.

17TH & 18TH CENTURIES

The Baroque Suite

The different rhythms of the dances make them sound different — but they've got lots of <u>shared features</u>...

Most Baroque Dances are in Binary Form

1) Dances in binary form have <u>two bits</u> to the tune — Section A and Section B.
2) Each bit is <u>repeated</u>. A's played twice, then B's played twice — AABB.

| SECTION A first idea | SECTION B second, contrasting, idea |

3) Section B <u>contrasts</u> with Section A. The contrast's usually made by <u>modulating</u> to related keys (see P.30 of the Core book).
4) As a change composers sometimes <u>paired</u> binary form dances together, <u>repeating</u> the <u>first</u> at the <u>end</u>. This made an overall <u>ternary form</u> shape — Dance A, Dance B, Dance A.

| DANCE A first idea | DANCE B second, contrasting, idea | DANCE A first idea |

There are Regular Phrases and Obvious Cadences

1) Baroque dances tend to have <u>regular phrases</u>. Each phrase lasts the same number of bars — usually <u>four</u>.
2) The end of each section is clearly marked by an obvious <u>cadence</u> (see P.28 in the Core book).

I (D) V (A) → *imperfect cadence*

Listen Out for Fancy Ideas in the Rhythm and Tune

In the exam, if you can say <u>how</u> composers make their dance tunes and rhythms more interesting, you'll get better marks. Listen out for:

1) Simple, <u>repetitive rhythms</u> to emphasise the overall <u>character</u> of the dance.
2) <u>Hemiola</u> — a special kind of <u>syncopation</u>. It's sometimes used in <u>triple time</u> dances just before an important cadence. The strong beats are changed so that <u>2 bars of 3</u> (123, 123) cross over the bar lines to sound like <u>3 bars of 2</u> (12, 12, 12).
3) <u>Sequences</u> — a pattern in the tune is repeated but starts on a different note each time.
4) <u>Imitation</u> — a phrase is repeated with slight changes. Each phrase imitates the one before. Tunes can be passed around different instruments and then overlap.
5) <u>Ornaments</u> (e.g. grace notes and trills) are put in to make the tune more interesting.

Suites are Played by Orchestras or Harpsichords

Some suites are played by a solo harpsichord, but others are played by a Baroque orchestra. Baroque orchestras are way <u>smaller</u> than modern ones. This is a fairly typical line-up of instruments...

1) The main section is the strings — violins, violas, cellos and double bass.
2) The <u>bass line</u> and <u>harmony parts</u> are always played by a keyboard instrument like a harpsichord and a bass instrument like a cello. This is called the <u>basso continuo</u> — it's used in <u>all</u> Baroque instrumental pieces.
3) Other instruments around in the Baroque period were the <u>flute</u>, <u>oboe</u>, <u>bassoon</u>, <u>horn</u>, <u>trumpet</u> and <u>timpani</u>. These were added to the orchestra depending on the <u>occasion</u>, the patron's <u>cash flow</u> and the <u>availability</u> of players.
4) A <u>trio</u> of instruments, with two parts in the treble clef and one in the bass, is sometimes used as a contrast — especially in a ternary form minuet where Dance B is played by the trio.

Too many suites will rot your teeth...

A fave exam question is *Where would you hear this piece played?* With Baroque dances it's not too hard to work out. If the music's played by a <u>big orchestra</u> then the music's for a fancy, <u>outdoor royal occasion</u>. If it's played by a <u>smaller orchestra</u> or solo instruments it's written for playing <u>indoors</u> in a palace.

Ballroom Dances

No marks will be awarded for ball gowns, coiffure, sequins or rictus-grin.
However, <u>marks will be awarded</u> for your knowledge of musical aspects of the waltz and polka.

The Waltz Craze Started in Vienna

1) People first started writing and dancing waltzes in <u>Austria</u> — mostly in the ballrooms of <u>Vienna</u>.

2) The first waltzes were written in the <u>1790s</u>. The most famous waltz composers were the Strausses.

3) The waltz ended up being one of the most popular dances of the nineteenth century — not just in Vienna, but all over <u>Europe</u> and in <u>North America</u> too.

> There were lots of waltzing Strausses: the dad was <u>Johann Strauss the Elder</u>. He had three sons who all composed waltzes — <u>Johann</u>, <u>Josef</u> and <u>Eduard</u>.

4) People thought the waltz was really <u>saucy</u> at first — it was the first dance ever where people held each other so <u>closely</u>.

DADDY STRAUSS: *Johann I*

BABY STRAUSSES: *Eduard Johann II Josef*

...Apparently they all looked quite similar too. Although it's <u>just possible</u> I made that up so I didn't have to find pictures of all of them ;-)

The Rhythm Goes 'Oom Cha Cha, Oom Cha Cha'

1) A waltz is always in <u>triple metre</u>. The time signature's usually <u>3/4</u>.

2) The '<u>oom</u>' is <u>stronger</u> than the 'cha cha', so the rhythm <u>feels</u> more like <u>one beat in a bar</u> than three.

3) The 'oom cha cha' rhythm is emphasised in the <u>accompanying chords</u>.

OOM cha cha   OOM cha cha   OOM cha cha   OOM cha cha

4) Waltzes written for dancing have a <u>steady</u>, <u>constant</u> beat. Waltzes for listening often have <u>pauses</u> and use <u>tempo rubato</u>. (The beat of the music's pulled about — some bits go faster, some slower.)

The Chords are Simple and Don't Change Much

A waltz has a <u>strong clear tune</u>, closely backed by the chords. It's called a <u>homophonic texture</u> — see P.31 in the Core book for more on texture.

1) The chords are pretty simple — mostly they're the <u>primary chords</u> I, IV and V.

2) The same chord's used for <u>at least one bar</u>, and sometimes two or four bars.

3) <u>One note</u> of the chord's played on the 'oom'. On the 'cha cha' the <u>rest of the notes</u> are played together, or the whole chord's played.

4) The speed of chord changes is called the <u>harmonic rhythm</u>. Waltz chords change slowly, so waltzes have <u>slow</u> harmonic rhythm.

5) This slow, simple chord pattern can get a bit repetitive, so composers use <u>appoggiaturas</u> and <u>chromatic notes</u> to spice up their tunes (see core book, p27).

Here's a bit of a waltz by <u>Johann Strauss the Younger</u> (🙂)

Slurring over the bar adds a touch of <u>syncopation</u>. The accents in bar 3 add syncopation too.

This is a <u>chromatic appoggiatura</u> — A♯ doesn't belong in the key.

This is the <u>first note</u> of a <u>C chord</u>.

These are the rest of the notes in the <u>C chord</u>.

This in an <u>inverted G7 chord</u> with the <u>3rd in the bass</u>.

19TH CENTURY

Ballroom Dances

And-a <u>one</u>, <u>two</u>, <u>three</u>, one, two, three, one, two, three, one...

Waltzes Started Simple and Ended Up Complex

The first waltzes were written in <u>binary</u>
with two 8-bar repeated sections.

SECTION A	SECTION A repeated	SECTION B	SECTION B repeated

waltz 1	SECTION A	SECTION A repeated	SECTION B	SECTION B repeated
waltz 2	SECTION A	SECTION A repeated	SECTION B	SECTION B repeated
waltz 1	SECTION A	SECTION A repeated	SECTION B	SECTION B repeated

Then pairs of waltzes were
grouped together to make
<u>ternary form</u> pieces.

1) <u>Joseph Lanner</u> (another composer from Vienna) and <u>Johann Strauss the Elder</u> made waltzes even <u>longer</u> and more <u>complex</u>. They strung five or more waltz tunes together. Each tune lasts <u>16-32 bars</u> and is in <u>binary</u> or <u>ternary</u> form. They also added <u>slow introductions</u> and <u>codas</u>.
2) Johann (baby) Strauss wrote two of the most famous longer waltzes — *The Blue Danube* and *Tales from the Vienna Woods*.

Waltzes were Played by Big Orchestras

Waltzes and polkas were played by the <u>large orchestras</u> that were standard in the <u>Romantic period</u>.
There's a lot of <u>brass</u> and <u>woodwind</u>, including more unusual instruments like piccolos.
The percussion sections have a big <u>variety</u> of instruments, e.g. timpani, tambourine, triangle and snare drum.

Waltzes Spread Beyond the Ballrooms

1) Waltzes crop up as <u>dances</u> and <u>songs</u> in <u>operettas</u>. Some of the more famous ones are by <u>Johann Strauss the Younger</u> (e.g. *Die Fledermaus*) and <u>Gilbert and Sullivan</u> (e.g. *Pirates of Penzance*).
2) Waltzes were so popular in the nineteenth century that people liked to play them at home on the piano. <u>Chopin</u>, <u>Schumann</u>, <u>Brahms</u> and <u>Weber</u> all wrote tons of waltzes for playing at home, as well as harder virtuoso waltzes for concert pianists.
3) Some nineteenth century composers included waltzes in their <u>orchestral works</u>, e.g. Berlioz's *Symphonie Fantastique*, Tchaikovsky's *4th* and *5th Symphony*, and Ravel's *La Valse*.
4) Tchaikovsky put waltzes in his <u>ballets</u> too — *Swan Lake* and *Sleeping Beauty* both include waltz tunes.
5) In the twentieth century the waltz was used in a few <u>musicals</u>. There are waltzes in Cole Porter's *High Society* and Rogers and Hammerstein's *The Sound of Music*.

The Polka's Another Popular Ballroom Dance

1) The <u>polka</u> hit the ballroom scene a bit later than the waltz, in the 1830s, but ended up just as popular.
2) It was originally a <u>folk song</u> from Bohemia — that's the western part of the Czech Republic.
3) A polka has a lot more energy and jerkier movements than a waltz. Partners hold tight and move <u>quick-quick-slow</u>.
4) There are <u>2 beats per bar</u> and polkas are usually in 2/4. The polka rhythms often copy the dance movements.

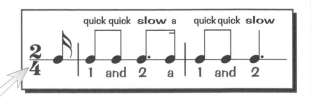

5) Just like waltzes, polkas were written in binary and ternary forms and composers used techniques like appoggiaturas to <u>spice up</u> the tunes.
6) The <u>baby Strausses</u> wrote lots of polkas with fancy <u>orchestral effects</u>. The most famous are the *Thunder and Lightning* and *Pizzicato Polkas*.
7) Like waltzes, polkas moved away from the ballroom and were used in <u>classical pieces</u>, e.g. in Smetana's opera *The Bartered Bride*.

The Club Scene

Modern club dance music's had all sorts of influences. Three of the big 'uns are <u>disco</u>, <u>rap</u> and <u>hip hop</u>.

Disco was the Dance Music of the 1970s

Before disco

DISCO

Disco first reared its groovy head in nightclubs in the <u>USA</u>.
The roots of disco were in <u>soul</u>, <u>jazz</u> and <u>funk</u>. Disco was
played in clubs and it <u>totally changed them</u>...

1) Until about the 1960s <u>audio equipment</u> was pretty ropey — you couldn't
   play a recording loud enough to dance to, so most clubs had live bands.

2) In the 1970s, <u>amplifiers</u>, <u>turntables</u> and <u>loudspeakers</u> got loads better.
   Suddenly you could play records loud enough to fill a club with sound.
   <u>DJs</u> took over from band leaders as the important people in a club.

3) People danced <u>on their own</u> rather than in pairs and they really enjoyed
   <u>showing off</u> their groovy dance moves and flashy outfits.

4) <u>Lighting technology</u> got more exciting too — <u>flashing lights</u> and <u>effects</u>
   became part and parcel of the experience of a night out in a club.

The Strong Beat and Catchy Tunes Made Disco Easy to Like

1) Disco tunes are almost always in <u>4/4</u>. They're played at around <u>120 beats per minute</u> (bpm).

2) The simple beat makes disco tunes really <u>easy to dance to</u> because just about any dance move
   will fit. People loved this because it gave them the freedom to make up their <u>own moves</u>.

3) People also liked the <u>catchy tunes</u>. Every disco tune has a <u>hook</u> — a short stab of <u>tune</u>,
   a <u>word</u> or a <u>phrase</u> that sticks in people's minds so they remember (and buy) the record.

Rap Grew out of Jamaican Reggae

Rap music started off in <u>Jamaica</u> in the late 1960s. Jamaican DJs started <u>talking</u> over
instrumental B-sides on reggae singles — they called it <u>toasting</u> or <u>dubbing</u>. They linked the
tracks with <u>drum machine</u> rhythms. The talking and drum machines <u>combined</u> to make early rap.

1) Rap got really popular in <u>American inner cities</u> in the <u>1970s</u>.

2) Rap <u>lyrics</u> were often about drug-taking, gangsters, police brutality and racism.
   It was a massive <u>contrast</u> to feel-good happy-clappy disco music.

3) Rap musicians often created <u>backing tracks</u> by <u>remixing</u> them from other songs.

4) Modern rap artists include <u>50 Cent</u>, <u>Eminem</u>, <u>Nelly</u> and <u>Notorious B.I.G.</u>.

Rap's had a Big Influence on Hip Hop

1) Like rap, hip hop's a dance style that came out of <u>street culture</u>.

2) It started out in the <u>New York Bronx</u> in the 1980s and is still popular today.

3) Hip hop uses rapping but overall it's more <u>tuneful</u>.

4) Hip hop tunes have a more formal <u>verse-chorus structure</u> than rap
   — more like disco.

5) <u>Graffiti art</u> and <u>break-dancing</u> are part of the hip hop culture.

6) <u>Missy Elliott</u> and <u>Ms Dynamite</u> are two famous female hip hop artists.

The Club Scene

Since the 1970s, tons of dance styles have developed.
The two important things they all have in common are <u>rhythm</u> and the use of <u>music technology</u>.

Club Dance Music Comes in Many Styles

Styles and names in club dance music <u>change</u> all the time. Here are a few basic definitions to get you started:

> **techno**   fast, hard beat, usually between 130 and 150 b.p.m., though can be much faster in hardcore techno. Rarely any voices or live sounds. Sounds mechanical and electronic.
>
> **jungle**   mega-fast tempo, often reaching 170 b.p.m. Drum-based. There are lots of short, fast notes called 'break beats' played between the main beats giving jungle a disjointed feel.
>
> **drum'n'bass**   a fusion of club dance music with jazz and funk (see P.44). Very heavy on the drums and bass.
>
> **UK garage**   dance music that uses ideas from jungle, drum'n'bass and modern rhythm and blues. Vocal sounds are used like percussion.
>
> **trance**   a very repetitive sound. Uses echoey and electronic sounds and lots of effects. Slow chord changes over a fast beat are meant to make you feel like you're in a trance.
>
> **ambient**   Slow, sometimes jazzy. Usually sounds chilled and spacial.

Just About All Club Dance Music Uses Music Technology

Music technology is the '<u>instrument</u>' of club dance music. Without it many pieces would be impossible to create. At a <u>live performance</u> in a club the DJ or MC plays <u>backing tracks</u> and then adds in <u>extra sounds</u>, with samples, keyboards or drum machine to build the piece up. They could do a bit of live rap too. In a <u>studio</u> a <u>producer</u> basically does the same thing — laying down a backing track then adding other sounds over it.

These are the main techniques used to create dance tracks:

1) *MIXING*   DJs work with <u>twin record decks</u> and <u>vinyl records</u>. Records with a <u>similar</u> number of <u>beats per minute</u> and in the <u>same key</u> are mixed together to create continuous dance music.

2) *SCRATCHING*   DJs turn records backwards and forwards by hand. The stylus makes a <u>scratchy</u> noise in the groove of the vinyl.

3) *SAMPLING*   This is using snippets of other people's <u>tunes</u>, <u>rhythms</u> or <u>voices</u> in your own music, e.g. JXL used an Elvis sample over their own backing track in *A Little Less Conversation*.

4) *LOOPING*   Recordings of short patterns of notes or rhythms, usually four bars long, are constantly <u>repeated</u> (looped) to make longer patterns.

5) *DIGITAL EFFECTS*   Special effects are used to create interesting sounds like <u>reverb</u> and <u>echo</u>. Another popular one is a <u>vocoder</u> which makes human voices sound like synthesised sounds.

6) *QUANTISING*   Computers can shift notes backwards and forwards to the nearest semiquaver, giving a track that's in <u>perfect time</u>. Lots of club dance tracks are quantised to make them sound <u>robotic</u>. <u>Groove quantising</u> is the opposite — it makes computer generated tracks sound more human.

7) *SEQUENCING*   This is a way of building up a song by recording lots of tracks one over another. It's usually done on a computer. The tracks could be electronic sounds, samples, real instruments and voices, synthesised instruments or a mixture of all these. This is sometimes called <u>multitracking</u>.

8) *REMIXING*   A remix is an <u>alternative version</u> of a piece of music. Pop and rock tunes are often remixed to turn them into dance music — they're speeded up and given a fast dance beat.

I want to see jungle on Come Dancing...

Well, club dance music is one thing most people will have no trouble spotting in the listening test.
If club dance music really isn't your bag and you don't know anything about it, find out <u>now</u>.

Dances of the Americas

Salsa is a tasty dip for tortilla chips. It's also a lively type of Latin American dance music which blends the 'son' style from Cuba with elements of jazz. The next few pages are about musical salsa.

Salsa Grew out of Son

The Spanish colonised Cuba and brought African slaves to work there on the sugar plantations. Over the years, music from the two cultures combined to make a dance style called son. Son is the main ingredient of salsa. Traditional son music has:

1) A basic repeated rhythm pattern called a clave (pronounced *CLAH-VEY*) played by hitting two sticks called claves (pronounced *CLAYVES*) together.
2) More repeated rhythm patterns played on percussion instruments like the maracas and bongos. These parts are often syncopated and form complicated cross-rhythms against the clave part.
3) Call and response (p36, Core book) between the lead singer (called the sonero) and the chorus (the choro).
4) Mainly primary chords (I, IV and V) in the harmony.
5) Harmonies in 3rds and 6ths.
6) The last note of a bar in the bass line often sets up the harmony for the following bar.

The Clave is the Key to any Son Tune

The clave is the basic rhythm of a piece of son music. It's the bit you tap your feet to. The son clave rhythm has a group of three notes and a group of two.

It goes like this...

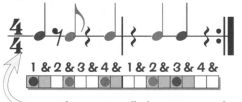

1 & 2 & 3 & 4 & 1 & 2 & 3 & 4 &

This one's called a 3-2 son clave.

...or like this...

1 & 2 & 3 & 4 & 1 & 2 & 3 & 4 &

This one's called a 2-3 son clave.

Have a go at clapping out the rhythm. Count out loud as you clap to make sure you're getting it right. Don't be surprised if you find it fairly tricky at first.

A piece of son music uses the same clave all the way through. All the other parts fit round it. This bit from the chorus of a song called "The Peanut Vendor" uses a 2-3 clave.

The clave rhythm isn't played in every single son tune — but you can still feel it in the rhythm of other parts like the bass line.

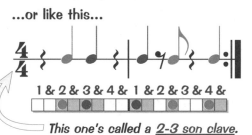

TUNE

2-3 SON CLAVE

BASS

There's a Special Clave for Rumba

There are different clave rhythm patterns to go with different dances. The clave for a rumba goes like this:

1 & 2 & 3 & 4 & 1 & 2 & 3 & 4 &

The rumba clave has a group of three and a group of two notes, just like the son clave — but the last note of the group of three is delayed by one quaver. It's a small difference, but has a big effect.

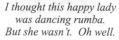

I thought this happy lady was dancing rumba. But she wasn't. Oh well.

Dances of the Americas

Son's the basic Cuban ingredient of salsa. In 1930s New York, son was mixed with big-band jazz. This was the beginning of salsa, which is now massively popular all over Latin America.

Big-Band Jazz Combined with Son to Make Salsa

In the 1930s, thousands of Cubans and Puerto Ricans migrated to New York. Musicians took bits of the American big-band jazz style and combined it with son — the result was salsa.

Salsa is basically son, with these features of big-band thrown in:

- *SYNCOPATION* — a lively offbeat rhythm
- *JAZZ CHORDS* — 7ths, 9ths and other chords with added or altered notes
- *RIFFS* — short repeated phrases
- *IMITATION* — one section of the band repeats a part just played by another section, e.g. the woodwind section might imitate a bit the brass section's just played
- *WALKING BASS LINES* — bass parts that move in crotchets, playing the notes of the chord with the odd passing note to fill the gaps
- *COMPING* — playing rhythmic chords on piano or guitar to accompany the tune.

The Salsa Band Combines Son and Big-Band Instruments

A traditional son band is called a sexteto. It has six instruments: guitar, string bass, bongos, maracas, claves and the tres, which is a bit like a guitar but with three strings.

As the salsa style developed and picked up influences from big-band, more instruments were added. These are the main sections in a modern salsa band:

FRONT LINE or HORNS

There are usually one or two trumpets or saxophones which play the tune.

VOCALS

There are one or two soneros (lead vocalists) and the choro (the chorus).

RHYTHM SECTION

This could have piano, guitar, bass and traditional Latin American percussion instruments like congas, timbales, bongos, maracas and the guiro. A standard drum kit is sometimes used too.

A Salsa Tune has Three Main Sections

There are three main chunks in a salsa tune. The three different chunks can appear in any order, and they can all be used more than once.

1) In the verse you hear the main tune, usually sung by the sonero or played by an instrumentalist.
2) The montuno is a kind of chorus where the sonero or lead instrumentalist improvises and the choro or other instrumentalists answer.
3) You'll also hear another section between choruses, called the mambo, with new musical material, e.g. different chords or a different tune. It's often played by the horn section. They either layer their parts to create a harmony, or stagger the parts, so one group plays and is quickly followed by another and another... You're also likely to hear an introduction and ending.
   There could also be a 'break' — a bit where the main tune butts out and just the rhythm section plays.

Here's a fairly typical salsa structure:

| INTRO | VERSE | BREAK | MONTUNO | MAMBO | MONTUNO | ENDING |

Dances of the Americas

Latin America is <u>bursting</u> with brilliant dance styles. The last two you need to learn are <u>samba</u> and <u>tango</u>.

Samba Comes from Brazil

1) Samba is a Brazilian <u>street carnival</u> dance.
2) It's played in either <u>2/4</u> or <u>4/4</u>. It sounds cheery and is played in a <u>major key</u>.
3) Samba instruments include a big variety of <u>percussion</u>, <u>Portuguese guitar</u> (a bright-sounding guitar with 12 strings), <u>keyboards</u> and, in larger street bands, <u>saxophones</u> and <u>trumpets</u>.
4) Samba is played by huge bands at carnivals, and by smaller bands for dancing <u>samba-salao</u> in ballrooms, or to accompany <u>samba-cancao</u> — samba songs.
5) Samba is often <u>mixed</u> with other dance styles, e.g. tango and rumba.

The Samba Beat Sounds like Springy Footsteps

1) The main samba beat is played by a pair of loud, resonant bass drums called <u>surdo drums</u>.
2) The basic surdo rhythm sounds like <u>steady marching footsteps</u>. The surdo players alternately hit the drum with a stick then damp it with the hand. This <u>muting</u> and <u>unmuting</u> gives the effect of short, <u>offbeat</u> springy notes in between the main beats.
3) Over the basic surdo beat you hear many other complex <u>syncopated</u>, <u>ostinato</u> rhythms.
4) One of the most obvious rhythms is played by the <u>agogo bells</u>. Other percussion to listen out for includes: <u>shakers</u> (known as *ganzas, caxixis* or *shekeres*), <u>scrapers</u> (the *reco reco*) and <u>tambourines</u> (*pandeiros*).

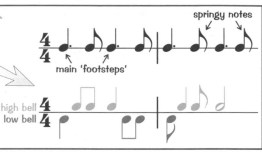

The Whistle Player is In Charge of a Samba Band

1) Large samba bands are controlled by a leader playing a two-toned <u>samba whistle</u>.
2) The whistle <u>sets the tempo</u> and signals <u>call and response</u> sections. In the call and response bits the whistle generally plays a rhythm and is answered by the rest of the band.

3) The call and response sections create <u>contrast</u> with the sections where everyone plays repeated rhythms.
4) Sometimes the whole band stops and then starts again. This is called a <u>break</u>.

Tango is a Sexy Dance from Argentina

Tango involves partners strutting about cheek to cheek and entwining their legs. These racy moves were frowned upon at first, but by the 1910s Argentina and Europe were <u>gripped by tangomania</u>.

1) Tango is in either <u>2/4</u> or <u>4/4</u>. It uses any of these basic rhythm patterns.
2) The exact line up of tango bands varies but listen out for any of these — <u>violin</u>, <u>piano</u>, <u>double bass</u> or a kind of accordion called the <u>bandoneon</u>.
3) Tango is still popular in Argentina today. Younger bands <u>fuse</u> the tango style with jazz, rock and club dance music.
4) <u>Twentieth century art music composers</u> have included tangos in their works, e.g. Stravinsky's *L'histoire du soldat* and William Walton's *Façade*.

I still don't understand why the drink's called Tango...

And another thing I want to know, is... if salsa and samba and all the other Latin American dances are popular with <u>everyone</u> over there, why is it that only <u>middle-aged divorcees</u> learn to do these dances over here?

Revision Summary

Blimey that's a big old list of questions. I think I'll just miss them out for now. I can remember most of the stuff in the section I reckon. I can always come back to this lot later, nearer the exams, can't I... Yeah, I think I'll just give revising a rest for now, go and watch telly... **OH NO YOU DON'T** — do these questions now. Then do them <u>again</u> nearer the exams. The more you test yourself with these, the better you'll know the section. And the better you'll do in your Listening test. And the more joyous you'll be when you get an A*.

1) Write a definition of metre (in music, not maths).
2) What is meant by the tempo of a piece of music?
3) Why don't you get lots of tempo changes in dance music?
4) Why are the phrase patterns in dance music regular?
5) What three types of event were Baroque dances played at?
6) Name two composers who wrote Baroque suites.
7) Describe the metre, tempo and mood of:
   a) a minuet   b) a sarabande   c) a gavotte   d) a gigue
8) Most baroque dances are in binary form — what's "binary form"?
9) Write down at least three ways Baroque composers made their tunes and rhythms more interesting.
10) Make a list of instruments that could be used in a Baroque orchestra.
11) What's "basso continuo"?
12) In what years was the waltz most popular?
13) Describe the rhythm of a waltz.
14) What does "tempo rubato" mean?
15) The texture of a waltz is homophonic — what does "homophonic" mean?
16) Explain three ways composers introduced variety into waltzes.
17) What was the structure of a typical early waltz?
18) What was different about the structure of later waltzes?
19) What kind of ensemble is a waltz most often played by?
20) What instrument did people use to play waltzes at home?
21) When did the polka become popular in ballrooms?
22) Describe the metre and movements of the polka.
23) Write out the basic rhythm for a polka.
24) Where did disco start up?
25) What made clubs that played disco different from earlier types of club?
26) Describe the disco rhythm and explain why it's easy to dance to.
27) What's a hook?
28) What's the usual structure for a disco song?
29) What two places did rap develop in?
30) Give a brief description of five club dance styles.
31) Name five ways that music technology is used in creating club dance tracks.
32) Write down six features of the Cuban son style.
33) Write out the son clave, either on a stave or with a box diagram.
34) What North American style combined with son to make salsa?
35) List the jazz ingredients of salsa.
36) What are the three sections of a piece of salsa music called?
37) Where's samba from?
38) What events is samba played at?
39) What are surdo drums? Write out the basic rhythm they play.
40) How is call and response used in samba?
41) Where's tango from?
42) Write out the three most common tango rhythms.

Music for Formal Occasions

Composers are sometimes commissioned to write music — maybe for a special occasion, like a coronation or something. They get paid for their work, but they have to stick strictly to what they've been asked to do.

Fanfares Sound like Something Important is Happening

1) They're usually played at <u>important events</u> such as <u>weddings</u>, <u>funerals</u> (especially <u>military</u> ones) and <u>coronations</u>.

2) They're used in films to mark the <u>arrival</u> of <u>kings and queens</u>.

3) They're often played on <u>brass</u> instruments (like <u>trumpets</u>) and <u>percussion</u>.

4) The tune's usually <u>simple</u> — using notes from <u>basic chords</u> and straightforward <u>rhythms</u>.

Example of a fanfare tune using only notes from C chord — C, E, G:

5) <u>Aaron Copland</u> was asked to write a <u>fanfare</u> in 1942 by the conductor Eugene Goosens to help with the <u>war effort</u>. The result was '<u>Fanfare for the Common Man</u>' (1943).

Composers Often have to Write Music to Fit Given Words

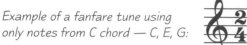

Operas contain Recitatives and Arias

1) <u>Operas</u> are secular works — that means they don't have anything to do with religion — they're basically <u>plays</u> that are <u>sung</u> instead of <u>spoken</u>.

2) An important part of <u>opera</u> is the <u>recitative</u>. This is where the <u>plot unfolds</u>. The <u>music</u> generally follows the <u>words</u>, not the other way round, and it's often used for conversations (see p40, core book).

3) <u>Arias</u> are written to give <u>solo singers</u> a chance to <u>show off</u> their skills.

4) The composer has to compose the <u>recitative</u> and <u>aria</u> according to the <u>mood</u> of the <u>character</u> who will be performing it.

Oratorios are like Operas but Religious

1) <u>Oratorios</u> are pretty much the same thing but <u>religious</u>.

2) Because the subject's usually very deep and meaningful, oratorios are a lot <u>less flashy</u> than operas.

3) The <u>words</u> are much <u>more important</u> than the <u>music</u>.

See page 40 of the core content book for more on operas and oratorios.

Odes are Poetry set to Music

1) <u>Poems</u> are often set to music for special events — these are called <u>odes</u>.

2) Odes are usually written in <u>praise</u> of someone or something, and they're used for things like <u>birthday celebrations</u> and <u>coronations</u>.

3) Elgar wrote '*Coronation Ode*' for the coronation of King Edward in 1902. The grand finale is '*Land of Hope and Glory*' — which is a very rousing, patriotic song, as you probably know.

NB Many poems are called odes but aren't meant to be set to music. You don't need to worry about them though.

Caesar, you're so great — but beware the odes of March...

So for the three 'O's (opera, oratorio and ode), the <u>words</u> are the really important bit. The music *HAS* to complement them as best it can. If it does it badly, the mood will be all wrong and it'll <u>spoil everything</u>.

Music for Formal Occasions

Overtures and Introductions Set the Mood for an Occasion

1) You usually hear an <u>organist</u> or <u>pianist</u> playing introductory music in a <u>church</u> as people are <u>coming in</u>. The music's usually <u>welcoming</u> and happy, and similar in style to the music that'll be played in the service.

2) An <u>overture</u> is an <u>introductory</u> piece of <u>music</u> for an <u>opera</u> or <u>play</u>. The point of it is to put the audience in the <u>right mood</u>, or (more cynically) to <u>shut them up</u> before the performance starts...

E.g. If the play was a tragedy, the music would be <u>dark</u> and <u>sombre</u>. If it was a <u>comedy</u>, it'd be a bit more <u>light-hearted</u> and <u>up-tempo</u>.

3) <u>Overtures</u> are also played before <u>dance suites</u>.

4) There are <u>endless possibilities</u> for styles of overture but there's a couple of types from the 17th century that it's kinda worth knowing about. Honest.

The French Overture

Slow	Fast	(Fugal) Slow

E.g. Beethoven's 'Consecration of the House', written as the overture to the music for the play 'The Ruins of Athens'

The Italian Overture

Fast	Slower	Fast

E.g. Alessandro Scarlatti's 'Dal male il bene'

Tips for Writing Your Own Play or Film Introduction
1) The <u>structure</u> of the music could just <u>follow</u> the structure of the <u>story</u>, e.g. happy-sad-funny-dramatic.
2) You could include <u>contrasting sections</u> where the <u>mood changes</u>. You may need to <u>modulate</u> into <u>different keys</u> to back up mood changes.
3) This is a good opportunity to write for loads of <u>instruments</u> and to do fancy things with <u>dynamics</u>.
4) You can write a special <u>motif</u> or <u>theme</u> to represent one of the <u>main characters</u>.
5) Or you could just <u>pick out the main mood</u> of the story.

See Section 2 on film music.

The National Anthem Represents our Queen and Country

1) The <u>National Anthem</u> is <u>played</u> at <u>events</u> that the <u>Queen</u> attends, and at events that represent the <u>country</u> such as <u>football matches</u>, Grands Prix, etc.
2) The tune is <u>simple</u> and uses lots of <u>repetition</u>. The <u>range</u> is easy for <u>most people</u> to <u>sing</u>.
3) The British National anthem sounds stately and grand. It's slow — slower than walking pace — which makes it feel like you could process grandly to it. If you get what I mean.
4) If not <u>sung</u>, the national anthem is usually <u>played</u> on <u>traditional orchestral instruments</u>.
5) But that's not always the case. At the <u>Queen's Golden Jubilee</u> in 2002, <u>Brian May</u> from the band <u>Queen</u> played it on <u>electric guitar</u> for the Jubilee <u>pop concert</u> — which made it appropriate for the day but still... well, jubileeish, I suppose.

That's Brian May, that is. No really it is. (And that's not a bass guitar... honest.)

There are Other Occasions you Could Write Music for...

Music for a School Award Day would be Formal and Happy

1) You might choose <u>orchestral instrumentation</u> or something <u>simple</u> like <u>piano</u> and <u>flute</u>.
2) You're better using a <u>major key</u> to show it's a <u>happy occasion</u>.
3) The <u>melody</u> and <u>harmony</u> might be <u>simple</u> and <u>memorable</u>.
4) A <u>moderate tempo</u> would make it feel <u>formal</u>.
5) Think about the <u>structure</u>. <u>ABA</u>'s good — <u>not too long</u> and with a <u>contrasting section</u> to keep it interesting.

Music for a Remembrance Service would be Sombre and Reflective

1) You'd probably choose a <u>minor key</u> — to be in keeping with the <u>sad mood</u>.
2) <u>Slow tempo</u> and <u>long notes</u> would create more <u>space</u> and give the congregation time to think.
3) A <u>monophonic</u> or <u>homophonic</u> texture could be used to continue with the <u>reflective</u> feel.
4) To keep the piece <u>simple</u> you might keep to just <u>one or two instruments</u>.

God save our gracious rugby team...

Ah... 2003... the year that'll go down in English sporting history. And where would we have been without Jupiter from Holst's *The Planets* to get us all back in the mood after the adverts, I ask you.

Music for Informal Occasions

Some Tunes are Meant to be used Over and Over Again

Everyone can Remember Happy Birthday

1) When people sing <u>Happy Birthday</u> they don't need any <u>backing</u> — but it could be played on pretty much any instrument that people have to hand.
2) <u>Everyone</u> can <u>remember</u> the <u>tune</u> — because it's so <u>simple</u> and <u>catchy</u>.

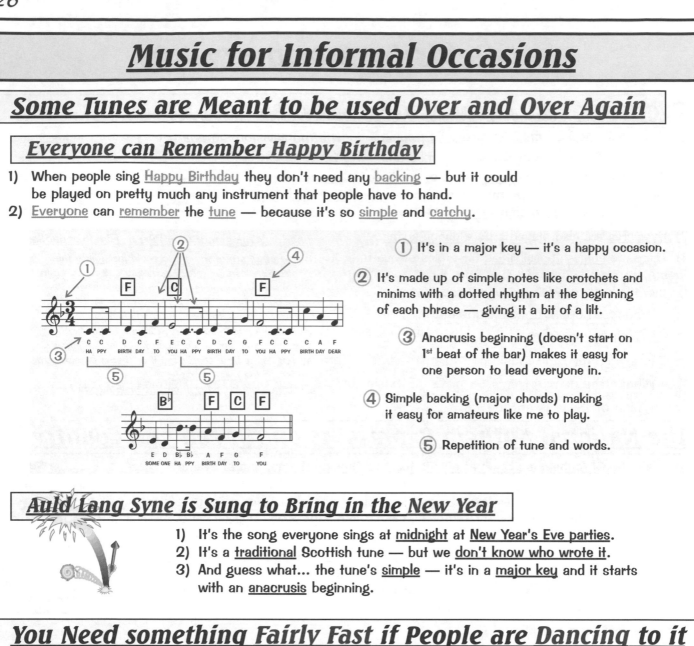

① It's in a major key — it's a happy occasion.

② It's made up of simple notes like crotchets and minims with a dotted rhythm at the beginning of each phrase — giving it a bit of a lilt.

③ Anacrusis beginning (doesn't start on 1st beat of the bar) makes it easy for one person to lead everyone in.

④ Simple backing (major chords) making it easy for amateurs like me to play.

⑤ Repetition of tune and words.

Auld Lang Syne is Sung to Bring in the New Year

1) It's the song everyone sings at <u>midnight</u> at <u>New Year's Eve parties</u>.
2) It's a <u>traditional</u> Scottish tune — but we <u>don't know who wrote it</u>.
3) And guess what... the tune's <u>simple</u> — it's in a <u>major key</u> and it starts with an <u>anacrusis</u> beginning.

You Need something Fairly Fast if People are Dancing to it

1) The usual <u>tempo</u> for dance music is about <u>120</u> to <u>180</u> <u>beats per minute</u>.
2) You'll need to use <u>popular dance rhythms</u> — <u>drum machines</u> or <u>samplers</u> might be used.
3) <u>Synthesised</u> sounds from <u>keyboards</u> would work better than acoustic instruments.
4) <u>Repetition</u>, <u>sequences</u> and <u>riffs</u> are all pretty essential in dance music.
5) It would be better to <u>pre-record</u> the music so you can control the levels and have lots of different <u>layers of sound</u>.
6) The ideal length for a modern dance tune is about <u>5 minutes</u>.
7) <u>Structure</u>'s important in dance music — the changes are often <u>subtle</u> and the <u>texture</u> becomes more <u>complicated</u> as the piece <u>builds</u>.
8) Whatever happens, the music should make you want to <u>move your feet</u> and shake your booty.

See pages 18-19 on the club scene.

Protest Songs are Meant to Change People's Minds

1) In the 1980s The Special AKA recorded a song called '<u>Free Nelson Mandela</u>' to help with the campaign to... you guessed it... free Nelson Mandela.
2) The song starts with <u>just voices</u> (a cappella) — which gives it an <u>African</u> feel.
3) The chorus is <u>one simple line</u> that's <u>repeated</u>. They really <u>hammer the point home</u>.

Does anyone ACTUALLY know the words to Auld Lang Syne...

Christmas, New Year, birthdays, general party-type things — for anything like that you want happy, simple music. Nothing too complicated or Joe Public just ain't gonna remember it.

Section Four — AoS3: Music for Special Events

Revision Summary

Dum... dada dum... dada dum dum dum dum dum dum dum dum dum... dad dum...
Yes, that means something important's happening. It's the revision summary.
Once again, it's a nice short section, so it shouldn't be too painful.

1) When are fanfares usually played?

2) What instruments might you expect a fanfare to be played on?

3) What fanfare did Aaron Copland write in 1943?

4) Why did he write it? (Apart from the money.)

5) What is an opera?

5a) Why is an opera? (trick question)

6) What's an aria?

7) In a recitative the music has to follow the rhythm of the _____.

8) What's the name given to a piece of music that's like an opera but religious?

9) Which of these is an ode?

   a) a bad smell, b) a poem set to music, or c) a poem set to a bad smell?

10) What's the name given to a piece of music that's played before an opera or a dance suite?

11) What kind of songs might be appropriate for an international sporting event between two countries?

12) For a joyous event would you write a song in a major or a minor key?

13) What kind of music would be appropriate for a funeral? Think about tempo and key.

14) List 5 reasons why Happy Birthday is such a great song.

15) What are the words to 'Auld Lang Syne'? (another trick question — I'm such a joker)

16) How fast should a song be if people are going to dance to it without falling asleep or doing themselves a permanent?

17) What's a protest song?

The Classical Orchestra

This AoS — *Orchestral Landmarks* — covers orchestral music in the Classical period, the Romantic period and the twentieth century. The Classical period came first, so that's what I'll start with here, I reckon.

Orchestral Music was Written for Wealthy Audiences

1) The Classical period begins in roughly 1750. At that time, composers worked for the top level of society — royalty, aristocrats and the church. They were paid to write music for official events, church services and plain old entertainment. Composers had to write music that their patrons (employers) would approve of.

2) Later in the Classical period society changed. Middle-class people had more money and wanted entertainment. They built public concert halls where they could go to listen to music.

3) Famous Classical composers like Haydn and Mozart worked for patrons, but they also put on concerts in the new concert halls. By the 1800s, composers could earn quite a bit of money from ticket sales at concert halls. This gave them more freedom — they could write for the tastes of concert-goers instead of just pleasing their patrons.

Classical Orchestras Mostly Used Stringed Instruments

In the Listening, they'll almost definitely ask you what kind of orchestra you're listening to — classical, romantic or twentieth century. The easiest way to tell is to work out what instruments you can hear.

1) Classical composers wrote for smallish orchestras.
2) This is a fairly typical layout for a classical orchestra:
3) The most important section is the strings. They're the dominant sound in all Classical music. The violins generally play most of the tunes.
4) The wind instruments play extra notes to fill out the harmony. When they do get the tune, they mostly just double the string parts.
5) You do hear the odd wind solo. Orchestral pieces called concertos (see p30) feature one solo instrument accompanied by an orchestra.

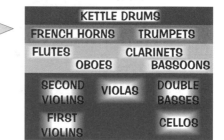

To get the flavour of Classical style listen to Haydn's London Symphonies (nos. 96–104), written between 1791 and 1795.
Here's a bit from no. 101, *The Clock*.

Wind instruments have long, held harmony notes.
If they do get the tune (like the flutes do here), it's usually just doubling up the string parts (here it's the first violin part).

The strings are the busiest.
The first violins have the tune.

The earliest Classical music uses a harpsichord to fill in harmonies (like in Baroque music, see P.15) but Classical composers eventually stopped using it.

Flute · Oboe · Clarinet · Bassoon · Horns & Trumpets · Timpani · First Violins · Second Violins · Violas · Double Bass & Harpsichord

I find wind more uncomfortable than harmonious...

Here's a handy tip: the key to the Classical orchestra is balance — which makes for a very clean sound. If the music's dominated by the brass or the percussion, the piece you're listening to is probably not Classical.

The Classical Style

A whole <u>pageful</u> of ways you can spot a Classical piece of music... enjoy.

Classical Music Has a Clear Simple Structure

Classical music sounds <u>clearer</u> and <u>simpler</u> than music from other periods. Partly this is because the tunes are structured in a very straightforward way, with <u>short</u>, <u>balanced</u> 2- or 4-bar phrases.

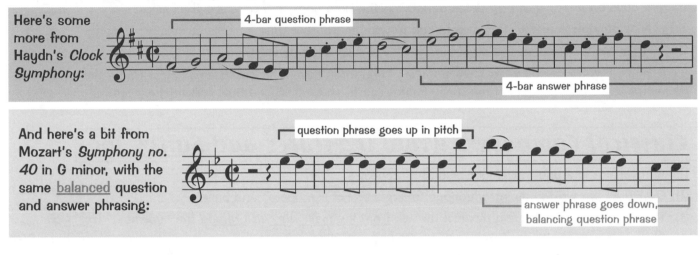

Classical Textures are Mainly Tune and Chords

1) Most Classical music has just <u>one tune</u> with <u>accompanying chords</u>. This makes the tune really stand out. It's called <u>homophonic texture</u> (see P.31, Core book).
2) These accompanying chords can be played in <u>different ways</u>:

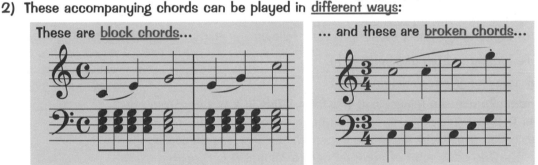

3) <u>Polyphony</u> — where <u>several tunes</u> weave in and out of each other — is used too, but not so often.

Classical Music Uses Major and Minor Keys

Classical music's always in either a major or minor key — the <u>tonality</u> is major or minor. <u>Bright</u>, <u>cheery</u> bits are in major keys and <u>gloomy</u>, <u>sad</u> bits are in minor keys. And...

...classical harmony is what's known as <u>diatonic</u> — nearly <u>all</u> the notes belong to the <u>main key</u>.

The Beat is Obvious and Easy to Follow

1) The <u>metre</u> in Classical music is very regular. You can happily <u>tap your foot</u> in time to the music.
2) The <u>tempo</u> stays <u>constant</u> — the speed of the beat stays pretty much the same all the way through, without massively speeding up or slowing down.

Classical style — a wig, tailcoat and breeches...

The best way to get good at <u>spotting</u> Classical music in the Listening test is to <u>listen</u> to lots of Classical music. The other thing you'll need to do is learn the main features from this page, so you can <u>explain</u> how you know that what you're listening to is Classical. Don't just read the page — make a <u>list</u> and learn it.

Classical Structures

This is one of the few pages (maybe the only one) in the book that you don't need to learn by heart — look things up here when you need to. It's all about how Classical composers planned their work.

Symphonies and Concertos are Popular Classical Forms

Symphonies and concertos were by far the most common works written for orchestra in the Classical period. They're covered in finger-licking detail on P.39 in the Core book, but here are the basics:

1) A symphony is a four-movement work played by an orchestra.
2) A concerto is a three-movement work for a soloist and orchestra.

Piano and violin concertos were most popular. They often have a bit called a cadenza, where the orchestra stops and the soloist manically improvises to show everyone how brilliant they are.

Classical Composers Wrote Overtures and Suites Too

1) An overture is a one-movement piece for orchestra.
2) Overtures are written as introductions to larger works like operas and ballets.
3) They use ideas, moods and musical themes from the main work to prepare the audience.
4) Classical orchestral suites are another offshoot of ballets and operas.
5) A suite is a collection of the incidental music used to accompany the action on stage, put together as a separate piece of music and played at concerts.

These are a bit different from Romantic overtures — see P.33.

Classical Composers Loved to Plan

Classical composers thought getting the structure and form right was one of the most important aspects of composing. Their music generally follows set plans.

See Section Five in the Core book if you want to find out more about sonata, ternary, variation and rondo.

1) First movements are mostly written in sonata form.
2) Second movements use ternary or variation form.
3) Third movements normally use the Minuet and Trio form. This is a ternary form structure so it goes A–B–A. A is a Minuet — a Baroque dance in stately 3/4 time. B is another minuet called a Trio. In the Baroque period, the Trio was played by three instruments. The Trio adds a bit of contrast before Minuet A is repeated.
4) Fourth movements use sonata, variation or rondo forms.

Musical Signposts Tell You What's Coming Next

The most obvious clue that a new section is starting in Classical music is a change of key. Classical composers were also keen on dropping advance hints that a new section was about to start. These hints are called musical signposts. They're not all that easy to spot at first, but with a bit of practice you should get the hang of it:

1) Bridge passages lead smoothly into the new theme.
2) Cadences clearly mark the end of a phrase or section. They sometimes come at the end of a piece too. When they do, the chords used in the cadence are repeated several times, to let the audience know it's all over.

Arches, columns, pediments, porticoes, amphitheatres...

Zippedeedooda, Zippedeeay, My oh my... what's that you say... I'm meant to be writing a revision guide, not just singing nonsense songs with nonsense words... Well my agent told me this was a singing job, so I'll darn well sing... Zippedeedoo... Hey, no need to get shirty... OW, that hurts... OK, I'm off...

Late Classical — Beethoven's Orchestra

In about 1800, Classical music started to sound quite different. The composer who introduced a lot of the changes was Beethoven. Even if you don't much like Classical music you might like Beethoven.

Beethoven is Part-Classical and Part-Romantic

The heading at the top of the page says "Late Classical" but you could also call Beethoven an early Romantic composer — his work bridges the two periods. His first four symphonies were written for a Classical orchestra (see P.28), but after that he started trying out all kinds of new stuff...

Beethoven Added Instruments to the Classical Orchestra

Beethoven created a bigger sound by adding more instruments to the Classical orchestra.
The new instruments didn't all play in every single piece — Beethoven just used them from time to time.

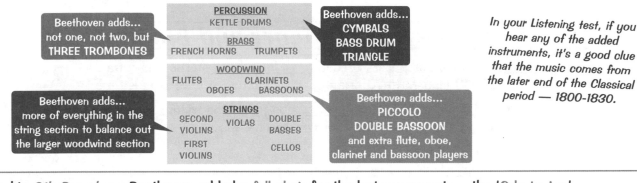

Beethoven adds...
not one, not two, but
THREE TROMBONES

Beethoven adds...
more of everything in the
string section to balance out
the larger woodwind section

PERCUSSION
KETTLE DRUMS

BRASS
FRENCH HORNS   TRUMPETS

WOODWIND
FLUTES   CLARINETS
    OBOES   BASSOONS

STRINGS
SECOND   VIOLAS   DOUBLE
VIOLINS   BASSES
FIRST   CELLOS
VIOLINS

Beethoven adds...
CYMBALS
BASS DRUM
TRIANGLE

Beethoven adds...
PICCOLO
DOUBLE BASSOON
and extra flute, oboe,
clarinet and bassoon players

In your Listening test, if you
hear any of the added
instruments, it's a good clue
that the music comes from
the later end of the Classical
period — 1800-1830.

In his 9th Symphony Beethoven added a full choir for the last movement — the 'Ode to Joy'.

Beethoven's Work Sounds Exciting and Dramatic

The structures of Beethoven's symphonies are Classical — they're the same structures used by Mozart and Haydn. The music sounds very different though — the earlier Classical music sounds light and elegant, but Beethoven's is full of tension and drama.

1) He uses contrasting sections of the orchestra,
   e.g. the brass playing against the strings.
2) There are big variations in the dynamics.
3) The rhythm drives the music forward.
4) Beethoven's orchestral works have powerful themes.
   The theme in the 5th Symphony is a great example. It goes like this:
   The theme (or motif) is used in all four movements. In the first movement it sounds like a threat but by the end it sounds like jubilation. Beethoven was the first to link the movements of a symphony in this way.

Beethoven Paints Pictures with the Music

Beethoven's music is often designed to create pictures. In the 6th Symphony (also called The Pastoral) the music makes you feel like you're in the countryside. It's easy to imagine you can hear birdsong, the babbling brook, country dancing, thunder and lightning and the howling wind. This idea of painting pictures with music was pushed further with Romantic program music (see P.32-33).

True or false — Beethoven is Dutch for beetroot...

It's not too hard to spot a piece of Classical music but it gets trickier when you have to spot the difference between a piece by, say, Mozart and a piece by Beethoven. Learn the stuff on this page and LISTEN TO LOTS OF CDS. Listening is the only way to find out what this stuff sounds like.

The Romantic Orchestra

The Romantic period runs from about <u>1830</u> to <u>1900</u>. "Romantic" in music <u>doesn't</u> mean slushy cards, lovehearts, candles and roses — it means <u>passionate feelings</u> expressed through the music.

Romantic Music Describes Feelings

1) Romantic composers mostly wrote <u>program music</u> — music that tells a story. It's usually based on a feeling, book, painting or poem. The opposite of program music is <u>absolute music</u>, written for the beauty of the sounds alone, like in the Classical period.

2) Program music creates <u>pictures</u> with sound. Different sounds, e.g. woody clarinet, or birdlike flute, are called <u>tone colours</u>. Romantic composers used tone colours to create varied <u>moods</u> and <u>emotions</u>.

3) To get the tone colours just right, Romantic composers paid a lot of attention to the <u>orchestration</u>, i.e. deciding which instrument plays which bits of a tune.

The Romantic Orchestra Got Bigger and Bigger

To get <u>more tone colours</u> Romantic composers needed <u>more instruments</u>. The orchestra changed from an average 30-40 players to <u>70 or more</u>. New instruments were added too:

1) <u>Piccolo</u>, <u>cor anglais</u>, <u>bass clarinet</u> and <u>double bassoon</u> joined the wind. The newly invented <u>saxophone</u> was used from time to time too.

2) <u>Tuba</u> joined the <u>brass</u>.

3) <u>Cymbals</u>, <u>triangle</u>, <u>tubular bells</u> and <u>piano</u> joined the percussion.

4) <u>More string players</u> had to be brought in to balance out the sound from all the new instruments. The <u>harp</u> began to be used too.

Classical orchestras followed the leader — first violin or harpsichord — to keep in time. The bigger Romantic orchestras had to bring in <u>conductors</u> to keep everyone together.

Everyone Got to Play the Tune

In <u>Classical</u> music it's almost always the <u>strings</u> who get the <u>tune</u>, because it was easiest for them to play all the notes. Technical advances in the nineteenth century meant that <u>Romantic</u> composers could give the tune to just about <u>any instrument</u>.

1) The brass instruments they had in the Classical period didn't have <u>valves</u>. They couldn't play many notes, so in orchestral works they always ended up playing long harmony notes, never the tune. When valves came in, in the nineteenth century, trumpet and horn players could play <u>tunes</u>.

2) The new instruments in the woodwind and brass sections gave them a greater <u>range</u> of notes. Composers started to treat these sections as <u>separate ensembles</u> within the orchestra, giving them <u>important passages</u>.

3) To fill out the sound in loud wind passages the strings were often given <u>fast scales</u> and <u>arpeggios</u>.

The biggest overall change was that now <u>any instrument</u> could get a <u>solo</u>, depending on the effect the composer was after. In the past it was only ever strings who got solos (except in concertos, where the main solo instrument might be a wind instrument, e.g. flute).

Romantic Tunes Sound Very Emotional

1) Romantic melodies are usually <u>longer</u> than Classical ones.

2) Nearly all express some sort of emotion and make you want to <u>sing along</u>.

3) Some tunes are <u>sad and melancholy</u>, others are <u>strong and victorious</u>.

The Romantic composers cranked up the emotion with lots of <u>chromatic notes</u>. These are notes from outside the key (e.g. G# in C major) which really spice up chords and harmonies. Another way of building and changing the mood was to have frequent <u>modulations</u> (key changes). If you get a piece of music in the Listening test and it seems to keep shifting key, you can be pretty sure it's <u>Romantic</u>.

The Romantic Orchestra

When Romantic music started to take over from Classical, people didn't just go, "That's nice dear," and carry on knitting. They were stunned and a bit shocked at all that <u>emotion</u> flying about. It was like a <u>revolution</u>.

Romantic Music is More Varied than Classical

There are more <u>quick</u>, <u>dramatic</u> changes in Romantic music than in Classical. Obvious things to listen for are:

1) A MASSIVE RANGE OF DYNAMICS — within one bar you could start *ppp* (very, very, very quiet), have a sudden, loud *sforzando* in the middle and go back to *ppp*.

2) EXPRESSION MARKINGS — the music's marked with instructions like *dolce* (sweetly), *amoroso* (lovingly), or *agitato* (agitated).

3) TEMPO CHANGES — you're likely to hear lots of tempo changes and *rubato* (bits where the players slow down in one bit, then go faster to make up for it later).

4) CHANGES IN TEXTURE — the <u>number of players</u> and the way their parts <u>weave together</u> changes throughout a piece.

This is Berlioz's main theme from the first movement of Symphonie Fantastique. *It's packed with extra instructions.*

Romantic Composers Developed New Structures

Classical structures like the symphony have very <u>strict rules</u>. Romantic composers wanted to concentrate on <u>expressing themselves</u>, not following rules, so they thought up new ways of organising their music:

CONCERT OVERTURE
A <u>one-movement</u> piece in <u>sonata form</u> (p38, core book). E.g. *Fingal's Cave* by Mendelssohn, Tchaikovsky's *1812 Overture* and *Romeo and Juliet*.

SYMPHONIC POEM
sometimes called a tone poem

A <u>large</u>, <u>one-movement</u> piece, often using a <u>single theme</u> which develops all through the piece. A good example is Liszt's *Les Preludes*.

PROGRAM SYMPHONY
A work with <u>several movements</u> based on a <u>story</u> or poem. Each movement tells a new bit of the story. Berlioz's *Symphonie Fantastique* describes a tragic love story. The fourth movement's called 'March to the Scaffold' — the main character dreams he has murdered his lover and has to face the guillotine. Cheery stuff.

INCIDENTAL MUSIC
This is played <u>between the acts</u> of a play. The music reflects the action on stage, a bit like film and TV music today (see Section 2). Romantic examples are Bizet's *L'Arlesienne* and Grieg's *Peer Gynt*.

Lots of Romantic Composers Wrote Nationalist Music

<u>National pride</u> was a big deal to the Romantics and lots of them used <u>dance rhythms</u> and <u>folk tunes</u> from their countries in their music. The nationalist bits are sometimes quite subtle, and sometimes not at all subtle — in the *1812 Overture*, Tchaikovsky, who was half-French and half-Russian, used the French and Russian <u>national anthems</u>.

Stop moaning — you'll get no symphony from me...

I feel sorry for people who played in orchestras round the beginning of the nineteenth century. Suddenly they had to do <u>emotion</u> and deal with all those <u>chromatics</u>. Not like the good old Classical days.

Twentieth Century Orchestral Music

Twentieth century music is a really mixed bag — everything from pretty tunes to weird ear-crunching brain-frying stuff. You <u>definitely</u> need to listen to examples to get your head round the weirder stuff.

More People Could Listen to Orchestral Music

1) The <u>gramophone</u> was invented in 1887. <u>Radio</u> and <u>TV</u> followed in the twentieth century.

2) People didn't have to travel to expensive concerts to hear orchestras play any more — they could listen to <u>records</u> and <u>concerts</u> at home. The audience for orchestral music was <u>bigger</u> than it had ever been.

Composers Used Orchestral Instruments in New Ways

Some twentieth century composers wrote for large <u>Romantic-style orchestras</u> with big percussion sections, pianos and harps. Others rebelled against big orchestras and started writing for smaller <u>chamber</u> orchestras.

They carried on using mostly <u>traditional instruments</u> but they experimented with different sounds and effects. This is the kind of thing you could hear...

PERCUSSION
* Different ways of hitting instruments, e.g. with <u>soft sticks</u>, <u>hard sticks</u> or <u>brushes</u>
* <u>Special effects</u> like playing cymbals on top of timpani or scraping a coin down the side of a cymbal
* Instruments from <u>beyond Europe</u> — e.g. bells and gongs from the Far East, African drums, Latin American bongoes, congas, guiros, maracas, claves and timbales

WIND
* <u>Flutter-tonguing</u> — making a 'r-r-r' sound while blowing
* <u>Breathy sounds</u>
* <u>Clicking keys</u> or <u>rattling valves</u>
* <u>Blowing</u> the <u>reed</u> or <u>mouthpiece</u> separate from the instrument
* <u>Singing</u> at the same time as playing
* Playing <u>multiphonics</u> — a special way of sounding two or more notes at the same time on one instrument, so that it sounds a bit distorted.
* <u>Glissando</u> — sliding from one note to another
* <u>Pitch bending</u> — the note is played just above or below actual pitch
* Using <u>mutes</u> — bunging a mute up the end of the instrument to change the sound

STRINGS
* A <u>mute</u> over the bridge (the bit of wood holding the strings up) — creating a distant, soft sound.
* <u>Vibrato</u> — vibrating the finger on the string to make wobbly-sounding notes
* <u>Tremolo</u> — moving the bow incredibly fast to make a dramatic sound
* <u>Sul ponticello</u> — playing near the bridge to make a high-pitched spooky sound
* <u>Harmonics</u> — high-pitched, distant sounding notes
* <u>Pizzicato</u> — plucking the strings
* <u>Tapping</u> on the <u>body of the instrument</u> with bow or fingertips

You don't need to learn all these examples, just read through them so you have a good idea of what <u>could</u> come up.

Composers Experimented with Different Sounds

If you hear <u>non-instrumental sounds</u> played alongside traditional instruments, it's a dead giveaway that you're listening to a twentieth century piece.

1) Composers used typewriters, car horns, iron chains, wind machines, recorded heartbeats, spoons, sandpaper... anything that they thought <u>sounded interesting</u>.

2) In the second half of the twentieth century some composers started to experiment with <u>electronic sounds</u>. They often used <u>recorded sound</u> alongside live sounds.

... any second now...

Twentieth Century Orchestral Music

Most of this stuff is the opposite of easy listening... I think that makes it good...

Twentieth Century Tunes and Harmony are Dissonant

In the Classical and Romantic periods the tune was pretty important. In the twentieth century things changed. Often tunes were made up of short fragments rather than being long and flowing. Sometimes there was no tune at all — instead it was rhythm and texture that were the main interest of a piece.

A lot of twentieth century music has wide leaps between notes. These leaps are often dissonant — not very tuneful at all.

Bruckner, Ninth Symphony

The harmonies were often dissonant too:

1) Some pieces were bitonal — two parts are played at the same time but in different keys.
2) Other pieces were completely atonal. There's no main key — no one note is more important than another. This is the complete opposite of tonal music — major and minor stuff — where the music always moves back to the tonic chord (the first chord of the scale).
3) Note clusters add more clashing notes. A note cluster is a chord with all the notes next to each other. Press your fist down on the piano and you'll get the idea...

The Rhythm is Often Syncopated and Irregular

You don't often hear a regular beat in twentieth century music — you're more likely to hear...

1) Syncopation — accents on the offbeat.
2) Polyrhythms — more than one rhythm playing at the same time, e.g. a 4/4 march and a 3/4 waltz.
3) Ostinati — constantly repeated rhythms. If they're relentless and chugging they're called 'motor rhythms'.
4) Metre changes — in one bar you're counting 3, the next 5, then 2...

Stravinsky was well into these two.

There's Loads of Different Styles...

You won't be asked to name the different twentieth century styles in the exam, but you do need a general idea of the different kinds of stuff written for orchestra. Here's a quick overview:

impressionism   Dreamy, mystical, floaty sounding music. Name comes from Impressionist paintings, which have a blurred 'out-of-focus' effect. Often uses a whole tone scale (P.17 in the Core book) and chords with added notes — 7ths, 9ths and even 13ths. The best examples are by Debussy — listen to his *La Mer* or *L'Apres Midi d'un Faune*.

twentieth century nationalism   The nationalist trend from the Romantic period continued. Rhythmic patterns and tunes give you the flavour of a particular country, e.g. the American cowboy tunes in Aaron Copland's *Rodeo* and English folk song in Vaughan Williams' *Fantasia on Greensleeves*. *Greensleeves* is also used in the 4th movement of Holst's *St Paul's Suite*.

neoclassicism   Composers looked back to the Classical period for ideas, writing symphonies for chamber orchestras, e.g. *Symphony of Psalms* by Stravinsky. Neoclassical music has the feel of Classical music but with twentieth century elements like bitonal tunes and motor rhythms.

serialism   This is a composing system invented by Schoenberg. The composer creates a tone row — a twelve-note series using all twelve chromatic notes. The whole composition is based on the tone row. Schoenberg's *Variations for Orchestra Op.31* is a good example to listen to.

aleatoric music   This is 'chance' music — the final decision about what to play is made in performance so the same piece sounds different every time it's played. E.g. in John Cage's *Music of Changes* the performers toss coins to choose which passage to play next.

jazz influence   Jazz elements like lively rhythms, syncopation, blue notes and muted brass were used in many twentieth century pieces. Have a listen to Gershwin's *Rhapsody in Blue* or *American in Paris*.

For the times, they are a-changing...

This section's all about how orchestras and orchestral music changed over the years. You'll have to learn Classical, Romantic and Twentieth Century really well so you can compare one with another.

Revision Summary Grid

For one day only I am being _nice_. I'm not going to put in the usual nasty, mean slimy test. Instead I've gone wild and created something never seen before in all the world, not in six continents nor on the seven seas. It's... a Revision Grid. Use it to _test yourself_. The examiners are definitely going to ask you how orchestras and music for orchestras changed over the four periods in this Area of Study — all the information you need to answer the questions is here. Learn one column at a time, and then one row at a time, until you've got the whole shebang _embedded in your brain_.

	CLASSICAL	LATE CLASSICAL	ROMANTIC	TWENTIETH CENTURY
DATE	1750-1800	1800-1830	1830-1900	1900-2000
ORCHESTRA & RESOURCES	Small scale orchestra. Strings dominate tunes.	Expanded orchestra — trombones, double bassoons, piccolos, extra strings and horns.	Very large orchestras with more varied percussion.	Large and small orchestras. Non-instrumental and electronic sounds. Traditional instruments played in new ways.
MELODY	Balanced, clear two- or four-bar phrases. Elegant and light.	Dramatic sound. Single theme used throughout most works.	Long, singable tunes. Often build to a climax.	Very varied. Wide leaps over dissonant gaps. Fragmented — notes dotted around different parts.
HARMONY & TONALITY	Mostly diatonic harmony. Always in major or minor key. Clear cadences.	Mostly diatonic harmony. Always in major or minor key. Clear cadences.	Lots of chromatic notes. Lots of modulation.	Key often not clear. Extreme dissonance. Bitonality and atonality common.
RHYTHM	Clear rhythms. Constant tempo and metre.	Driving rhythms.	Lots of tempo changes and rubato. Some syncopation.	Metre and tempo change often. Polyrhythm. Ostinato.
TEXTURE	Mostly homophonic. Occasional polyphony.	Mostly homophonic. Occasional polyphony.	Varied texture.	Huge contrasts in texture.

And by the way... it's no good just being able to parrot it — you've got to _understand_ it all too.

Voices in Pop

AoS5 takes those songs you know and love, analyses them in fine detail, then spits them out the other end as a dry, crumbly mass. Try and remember it's actually about something quite fun. Singing first...

The Lead Singer Sings the Main Tune

The lead singer (or vocalist) sings the main tune of a song.
If you get a pop song in the Listening test, definitely say something about the lead vocalist's style.
It's even worth mentioning really obvious stuff like whether the singer's male or female.

Backing Singers Sing the Harmonies

The backing vocalists are the ones who sing the harmonies.
These are the main ways backing singers do their thing:

| IN HARMONY all singing different notes | IN UNISON all singing the same notes | DESCANT singing a higher part in time with the main tune | CALL AND RESPONSE repeating whatever the lead vocalist sings or answering the lead with another tune |

Singers can do All Sorts of Fancy Stuff

There's more than one way to skin a platypus, and more than one way to sing a song.
Make sure you can describe exactly what you're hearing. Listen out for...

1) *A CAPPELLA* — singing with no instrumental backing.
2) *VIBRATO* — when singers quiver up and down slightly in pitch. It makes the voice sound warmer and more expressive.
3) *FALSETTO* — when men make their voices go really high. The BeeGees and Michael Jackson do this a lot.
4) *PORTAMENTO* — when a singer slides from one note to another.
5) *SCAT SINGING* — improvising using "doo" and "dat" sounds.
6) *RIFFING* — when singers decorate and add bits to the tune. They often go up and down a scale before coming to rest on one note. Riffing usually comes at the end of a phrase, between sections or to finish the song. You'll definitely have heard Whitney Houston, Mariah Carey and Céline Dion riffing.

Electronic Effects can be Added to Vocal Parts

Another way to make the singer's voice sound more interesting (or just weird) is to add electronic effects.

1) *REVERB* (short for reverberation) gives the voice a bigger sound — a bit like the effect you get when you sing in the bath.
2) *MULTITRACKING* makes it sound like there's more than one singer. With multitracking, one singer can record all the vocal parts in their song.
3) *SAMPLING* lets you bring in another singer's voice. A sample of someone else singing is dropped into the song. This one's nice and easy to spot in the Listening.
4) A *VOCODER* is equipment which electronically alters the singer's voice. It works the same way as adjusting notes on a keyboard.

I'm singing in the shower, just singing in the shower...

Last year I went to the annual Combined Examination Boards Music Examiners' Christmas Dinner and Disco. It was a joy to see all those examiners jiggling about in their corduroy trousers. They had a fine old time. After every song they all compared notes on the singing techniques and electronic effects.

Instruments of Pop

Along with the voice, most pop songs use a standard line-up of instruments...

Lead Guitar Plays Tunes, Rhythm Guitar Plays Chords

1) The lead guitarists play improvised solos in the instrumental sections. They also add in short fancy bits all the way through to decorate the tune.

2) Rhythm guitarists fill in the harmony all through the song. They either strum chords or pick out broken or arpeggiated chord patterns to a rhythmic riff (see P.36 in the core book). Different pop styles tend to use different kinds of riff.

The Bass Guitar Plays the Bass Lines

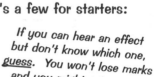

1) The bass guitar plays the lowest notes.

2) The player picks out individual notes, not chords, to play a low-sounding tune called the bass line.

3) You can play a glissando by sliding your finger up and down the string (this is easier on a fretless bass).

Electric Guitars can Play Effects

By plugging an electric guitar into an effects box you can get all sorts of effects. Here's a few for starters:

1) DISTORTION — a grungy, dirty sound.
2) FUZZ — fuzzy-sounding distortion.
3) CHORUS — makes it sound like more than one instrument's playing.
4) FLANGE — doubles up what the guitar's playing but shifts the phase of one bit, which can make it sound quite metallic.
5) WAH WAH — makes the guitar go, er... "wah wah".
6) COMPRESSION — evens out variations in volume.
7) PANNING — sends different sounds through different speakers. If you've got two guitarists trading solos, one could be panned left and one right to separate the sounds.

If you can hear an effect but don't know which one, guess. You won't lose marks and you might gain some.

The Drums Add the Rhythm

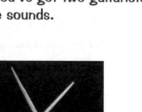

1) It's the drummer's job to set the tempo. They also play rhythms to fit the style of the song, just like the rhythm guitar.

2) The main instruments of a drum kit are snare drum, bass drum, high-hat, tom-toms and cymbals.

3) Drum pads or drum machines are often used to replace acoustic drums, or sometimes play alongside them.

Synthesisers can do Lots of Jobs

I'm not too keen on washing up.

1) Synthesisers (synths) can play any part.

2) Synths can make the sound of virtually any instrument you want, e.g. full string section or brass section.

3) They can play rhythmic chords, or solos and hook lines.

4) Most synths used for pop songs today are digital or soft synths. (See p57, core book for more on synths.)

5) Analogue synths were used in the 1970s and '80s (and made a bit of a comeback in the '90s). They're supposed to sound a bit warmer.

Pop will eat itself — probably with ketchup...

The examiners do like to ask a nice question about how the main tune interacts with the accompaniment. Don't just say which instruments are playing — write about how the accompaniment adds to the song.

Pop Song Structures

I like a bit of structure. Stops everything from dissolving into a shapeless horrible mess...

Most Pop Songs have a Verse-Chorus Structure

Pop tunes almost always start with an intro. It does two jobs —

* It grabs people's attention and sets the mood.
* It often uses the best bit from the rest of the song to make people sit up and listen.

After the intro, the structure of a pop song basically goes verse-chorus-verse-chorus...

* All the verses usually have the same tune, but the lyrics change for each verse.
* The chorus has a different tune from the verses, usually quite a catchy one. The lyrics and tune of the chorus don't change.
* In a lot of songs the verse and chorus are both 8 or 16 bars long.

This verse-chorus-verse structure is more poshly known as STROPHIC STRUCTURE.

The old verse-chorus thing can get repetitive. To avoid this most songs have a middle 8, or bridge, that sounds different. It's an 8-bar section in the middle of the song with new chords, new lyrics and a whole new feel.

The song ends with a coda or outro that's different to the verse and the chorus. You can use the coda for a big finish or to fade out gradually.

Other Common Song Structures Are...

CALL AND RESPONSE has two bits to it. Part 1 is the call — it asks a musical question. Part 2, the response, responds with an answer.

RIFFS can be used to build up a whole song. Each part, e.g. the drums or bass guitar, has its own riff. All the riffs fit together to make one section of the music. The riffs often change for the chorus.

See p36 of the core book for more on riffs.

BALLADS are songs that tell stories. Each verse has the same rhythm and same tune.

32-BAR SONG FORM breaks down into four 8-bar sections. Sections 1, 2 and 4 use the main theme. Section 3 uses a contrasting theme, making an AABA structure. The 32 bars are repeated like a chorus. The verse is only played once — it's usually slowish and acts more like an introduction.

...or half a pound of tuppenny rice — Pop goes the weasel...

These structures are easy-ish, but that doesn't mean you can go skimming through them. Make sure you've memorised all the different structures and the differences between them. And practise spotting them. Put the radio on when you're in the bath — you can stay in until you're shrivelled as a prune and call it revising.

Influences on Pop

This section's supposedly all about pop music since 1960, <u>but</u> there's some stuff that happened <u>before</u> 1960 that really can't be ignored. Without all this little lot, pop music could <u>never</u> have happened...

Blues has a Massive Influence on Pop Today

1) Blues music is a type of <u>Afro-American</u> folk song. The earliest blues songs were sung by <u>African slaves</u> working in terrible conditions on plantations in the USA.

2) In the early stuff, a solo singer is accompanied by <u>guitar</u> or <u>banjo</u> and the song lyrics are <u>slow</u> and <u>sad</u>.

3) When the blues hit American cities, singers were backed by <u>jazz instruments</u> like trumpets, clarinets, piano and double bass.

4) In the 1940s and 1950s a style called <u>rhythm'n'blues</u> (R'n'B) was developed. It's a <u>speeded-up</u> version of blues, played on <u>electric guitar</u> and <u>bass</u>.

5) Most blues songs and many pop songs are written to a pattern called the <u>12-bar blues</u>...

12-BAR BLUES
- The 12-bar blues pattern's in <u>4/4 time</u> and <u>12 bars</u> long.
- The only chords are <u>I</u>, <u>IV</u> and <u>V</u>.
- They're used in a <u>set pattern</u> through the 12 bars.
- The 12-bar structure is <u>repeated</u> all through the song.
- <u>Minor 7ths</u> are often added to the chords, e.g. C7 — CEGB♭, F7 — FACE♭, and G7 — GBDF. This makes the music sound even more bluesy.

BAR 1	BAR 2	BAR 3	BAR 4
Chord I	Chord I	Chord I	Chord I

BAR 5	BAR 6	BAR 7	BAR 8
Chord IV	Chord IV	Chord I	Chord I

BAR 9	BAR 10	BAR 11	BAR 12
Chord V	Chord IV	Chord I	Chord V
			Chord I

In Bar 12, you play chord V, <u>except</u> in the very last bar of the song, when you play <u>chord I</u>.

Bluesy Bass Lines Turn Up in Lots of Pop Songs

There are a few <u>bass lines</u> that started life in blues music which get used quite often in pop songs. Learn these two so you can spot them:

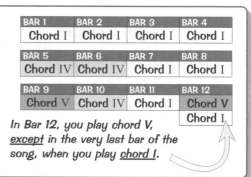

1) *WALKING BASS* moves in steady <u>one-beat notes</u> up and down the notes of chords I, IV and V.

2) *BOOGIE-WOOGIE BASS* is the same notes, played with <u>boogie-woogie</u> rhythm.

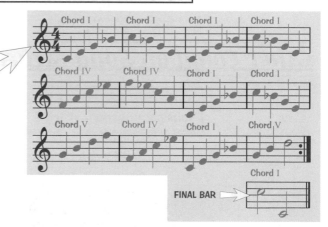

FINAL BAR

boo-gie woo-gie

The Blues and Loads of Pop Songs use Blue Notes

1) Blues notes are notes that are deliberately played flat. They add a <u>wistful</u> feel to the tune.

2) It's normally the <u>3rd</u> and <u>7th</u> notes of the major scale that get flattened, but sometimes the <u>5th</u> note's flattened too. So in C major, E, G and B are played as E♭, G♭ and B♭.

3) Blues notes can be played <u>as well as</u> the 'normal' notes of the scale, e.g. C-D-E♭-E-F-G♭-G-A-B♭-B-C, or <u>instead of</u> the standard notes, e.g. C-D-E♭-F-G-A-B♭-C.

I feel blue — blue as a blue-blooded bluebird stew...

The 12-bar blues pattern's dead old, practically <u>prehistoric</u>, but it's a great <u>starting point</u> for composing songs — play the chords through a few times, add a tune using the blues scale notes, throw in some lyrics and a drum beat and you've got a song. I'd call it <u>magic</u>, if magic wasn't so last year.

Influences on Pop

It wasn't just blues that helped to shape modern pop. Jazz, rock and roll and an obscure little English band called the Beatles all stuck their oars into the big fat cauldron of pop, too...

The Jazz Style Shaped Pop Music Too

You'll often hear these bits'n'pieces from jazz in pop songs:

IMPROVISATION
Performers make up their own bits of music based on a main tune or chord pattern.

CHROMATIC NOTES
Notes from outside the key are used in the tunes, e.g. D# in C major.

JAZZ INSTRUMENTS
Saxophones, trumpets and other jazz instruments came to pop through jazz.

CALL AND RESPONSE (see P.39)
This found its way into pop music via jazz.

JAZZ CHORDS
Chords with extra notes added, e.g. 2nds, 7ths, 9ths, 11ths and 13ths.

Rock'n'Roll Drove Kids (and Parents) Wild

Rock'n'roll created a major ruckus in the USA in the 1950s. Teenagers went mad for it, parents hated it and some went so far as to say it was evil. It can sound a bit tame today, but it's still worth a listen.

1) Rock and roll is a faster version of the 12-bar blues played on electric guitars.
2) The singing is country and western style.
3) Rock'n'roll has a really dancy feel.
4) Elvis Presley, Bill Haley and Jerry Lee Lewis all sang rock and roll.

The Beatles Have Influenced Most Bands Since the 1960s

The Beatles' style changed so much over the years that it's pretty hard to sum them up. They hit the charts in the 1960s and took popular music to a whole new level. Their music and image were totally different from anything that had come before.

1) The Beatles developed their own style by mixing black and white musical ideas like rock'n'roll, rhythm'n'blues, folk and ideas from classical music and non-western cultures.

2) They used pioneering recording techniques.

3) The *Sgt. Pepper's Lonely Hearts Club Band* album is a good example of all their ideas coming together. On 'The Benefit of Being Mr Kite' you can hear fairground sounds, 'Within Without You' uses Indian instruments like the sitar, and as a total contrast 'When I'm Sixty-four' is written in trad-jazz style.

Can you believe how cool we are?

Can a waxwork be cool?

4) Most people would agree that the Beatles' songs have stood the test of time and JUST ABOUT ALL POP MUSICIANS since then have been influenced by them.

5) The Beatles' influence is particularly noticeable in music by 90s Britpop bands like Oasis and Blur, and later Travis and Coldplay.

The Beatles — great songs, shame about the hair...

Someone you know is bound to have a massive record collection going right back to the Beatles, if not earlier. Buy them a big box of chocolates, go round to their house and listen to all their CDs and (gasp) LPs. It's the same for every topic in Music — it doesn't really make sense till you've listened to it.

Musicals

Musicals... love 'em or hate 'em, they're on the syllabus and they're here to stay...

Musicals are the Pop Version of Opera

1) Musicals are the pop version of opera (see P.40, Core book). They're performed on stage or film.
2) There's a fair bit of talking and dancing, but a lot of the story's told through singing.
3) An orchestra accompanies the singing and plays incidental music.
4) Musicals are generally written in the style of the pop music that's around at the time they're written.

The Musical was Invented in the USA

The first musicals were written in the United States in the early twentieth century.
Back then, they were called musical plays or musical comedies.

Probably the most famous Americans to write musicals were Rogers and Hammerstein. Richard Rogers wrote the music and Oscar Hammerstein wrote the words. If you've ever watched TV on Christmas Day you have definitely seen at least part of a Rogers and Hammerstein musical. They wrote Oklahoma, Carousel, The King and I, South Pacific and (my personal favourite) The Sound of Music.

Some Pop Songs Started Life in Musicals

Before rock and roll (i.e. before the 1950s) nearly all pop songs came from musicals.
Nowadays there are loads of different pop styles, but songs from musicals still hit the charts.
In the UK musicals by Andrew Lloyd Webber and Tim Rice have spawned a few chart hits:

- 'Memory' from *Cats*
- 'I Know Him So Well' from *Chess*
- 'Don't Cry For Me Argentina' from *Evita*
- 'No Matter What' from *Whistle Down the Wind* (sung by Boyzone)
- 'Whistle Down the Wind' from *Whistle Down the Wind* (sung by Tina Arena)

There are Four Basic Types of Musical Song

1) *SOLO CHARACTER SONG* — a character sings about how they're feeling —
   in love, full of hate, over the moon with happiness etc. 'Memory' from *Cats*
   and 'I Know Him So Well' from *Chess* are both solo character songs.
2) *DUET* — duets are basically the same as solo character songs, except there
   are two people singing so you get two different reactions to a situation.
3) *ACTION SONG* — the words of the song tell you what's going on in the plot —
   they lead you into the next bit of the story.
4) *CHORUS NUMBER* — the whole cast get together and have a big old sing-song.
   Like at the end of *Grease* — 'We go together like ramma lamma lamma ka dingedy ding de dong...'

All these styles of song developed from opera — solo songs are like arias and action songs are like recitative.

Once on a hill a lonely goatherd...

...was surprised to see a woman in a brown dress running towards him at full pelt, singing her lungs out.
If you find *The Sound of Music* just a bit too cute, try *West Side Story* by Leonard Bernstein. It's got great songs and the film version's got fantastic quiffs. Or see *Cabaret*. That's nothing like *The Sound of Music*.

Solo Ballads

Do you like Camembert... Then you'll <u>love</u> this page... I know I shouldn't let my personal prejudices cloud your pure-minded striving after the truth (and an A*) but I find ballads just a snifferette cheesy...

Ballads Tell Stories

1) <u>Ballads</u> have been around since at least the <u>fifteenth century</u>. Back then a ballad was a long song with lots of verses that told a <u>story</u>. It's the type of thing that was sung by <u>wandering minstrels</u>.

2) Modern <u>pop</u> and <u>rock</u> ballads still tell stories. Often they're <u>slow</u> and <u>sad</u> and tell some kind of <u>love story</u>. Songwriters like to put a romantic or spooky <u>twist</u> right at the <u>end</u> to keep people listening.

3) Each verse has the <u>same</u> rhythm and tune but different lyrics (see P.39 for more on this structure).

You'll hear ballads sung in many different styles — a <u>rock ballad</u> accompanied by <u>heavy drums</u> and <u>amplified guitars</u> sounds pretty different to, say, a <u>folk ballad</u> played on an <u>acoustic guitar</u>.

Singer-Songwriters Write Lots of Ballads

<u>Singer-songwriters</u> are artists who <u>write and sing</u> their own stuff. They tend to <u>accompany themselves</u> on either the <u>guitar</u> or <u>piano</u> and write a fair few ballads. The <u>style</u> of the ballads depends on the singer's own personal style. Here are a few performers who sing ballads — they all sound <u>very</u> different:

1) <u>Bob Dylan</u>'s most famous ballad is an <u>anti-war song</u> called 'Blowing in the Wind'. Bob sings a simple <u>major scale</u>, <u>diatonic tune</u> and accompanies himself on an <u>acoustic guitar</u> with simple strummed chords which give the song a folky feel (see P.46). All the verses have the same music and the same <u>last line</u> — 'The answer my friend is blowing in the wind, the answer is blowing in the wind'. The repeated line works like a <u>mini-chorus</u>.

2) <u>Elton John</u>'s 'Candle in the Wind' is a <u>love ballad</u> about Marilyn Monroe. Marilyn's real name was Norma Jean so the first line goes "Goodbye Norma Jean..." For Princess Diana's funeral he changed the words to "Goodbye English Rose..." Elton John accompanies most of his songs on the <u>piano</u>. His accompaniments combine <u>rhythmic chords</u> and <u>snippets of tune</u> — which is quite clever really because it stops things from getting boring.

3) <u>Sting</u> just about always writes his own songs. He accompanies himself on <u>bass guitar</u>, but he's also backed by his <u>band</u>. Sting's music takes a lot from <u>soul</u> and <u>jazz</u>. 'Seven Days' is a particularly jazzy ballad — it's in 5/4 time and uses jazzy major seventh chords.

4) <u>Kate Bush</u> bases the story of her ballad '<u>Wuthering Heights</u>' on the book with the same name. No one else in pop sounds quite like Kate Bush — she sings in a wailing, ghostly manner.

Ballads are Popular with Boy Bands and Girl Bands

<u>Boy bands</u> and <u>girl bands</u> played a big part in <u>1990s</u> pop and are still going strong. Bands like <u>Take That</u>, <u>Boyzone</u>, the <u>Spice Girls</u>, <u>Five</u>, <u>Westlife</u> and <u>Girls Aloud</u> are all marketed at young teenagers and they rely on their <u>image</u> as much as the music to shift CDs. <u>Emotional</u>, <u>slow</u> <u>ballads</u> are the perfect type of song to get fans to fall in love with the band (and buy their CDs).

Boy and girl band songs often use:

1) <u>Multitracking</u> in the chorus to <u>double up</u> voices and make the sound <u>fuller</u>.

2) Repeated, pre-recorded <u>hooks</u>.

3) Mostly <u>synthesised</u> sounds.

Borrow a lighter and wave it in the air...

Ballads should be really easy to spot, what with the tune being repeated over and over again. If you're a very emotional person and you often find yourself in <u>floods of tears</u> at the least excuse you'll have to steel yourself for the Listening Test — you can't go sobbing all over the exam papers. You'll put everyone else off.

Reggae, Soul & Funk

Reggae's a music style from Jamaica, and soul and funk started off in the United States. All three grew up in black communities in the late 1960s and the 1970s, but quickly ended up popular with just about everyone.

Reggae is Very Chilled

Reggae started in Jamaica in the 1970s. Probably the most famous reggae star is Bob Marley.

1) Reggae has a slow relaxed tempo and a light, offbeat feel. In most pop and rock the drums go bass, snare, bass, snare. In reggae they go snare, bass, snare, bass, giving an offbeat, relaxed feel.
2) The bass guitar part is loud and syncopated, adding to the offbeat feel.
3) Electric guitars play short, muted, offbeat riffs.
4) There are just 2 or 3 chords repeated all the way through the song.
5) Brass, saxophone, organ and backing singers are often used too.
6) You'll hear call and response between the lead singers, backing singers and instrumentalists.

Soul Music is the Pop Version of Gospel

Gospel is a singing style used in black churches in the USA. There's lots of improvisation, syncopation and call and response — the leader sings a line of a hymn and the congregation sings back in harmony. When soul records started to be recorded in the 1960s they were heavily influenced by gospel.

> **MOTOWN**
> The Tamla Motown record company was set up in Detroit in the 1960s. It was one of the first record companies to be run by black people and record mainly black artists. They recorded Diana Ross and the Supremes, Marvin Gaye and The Jackson Five. All Tamla Motown records have a similar sound:
>
> - *DOO-WOP HARMONIES* — backing vocals sung to nonsense words
> - *MULTITRACKING* — instruments, vocals and rhythm parts were recorded separately and played back together to create a thick wall of sound
> - *ORCHESTRAL INSTRUMENTS* — strings, brass and timpani are used for a fuller sound
> - *BACKBEAT RHYTHMS* — the accent falls on beats 2 and 4 of the bar
> - *TEENAGE LYRICS* — mostly about love
> - *HOOKS* — a line of the song is repeated over and over
> - *LOUD, SYNCOPATED BASS LINES*
> - *DANCY FEEL* — performers did set dance routines on stage
> - *LONG STRUCTURES* — instead of the usual AABA pop structure, ABABCC is more common

> **ATLANTIC SOUL**
> Atlantic Soul's more bluesy and rough-edged than Motown, with far less studio effects. Two massive soul stars were Aretha Franklin and James Brown. Atlantic soul has:
>
> - *A STANDARD LINE-UP* — guitar, bass, drums, organ, brass and backing singers
> - *SIMPLE CHORDS* — just a few simple chords in the accompaniment, often in 12-bar blues pattern
> - *SIMPLE TUNES* — but these are livened up with loads of gospel-style improvisation
> - *SEXY RISKY LYRICS* — they talk about heartbreak, dancing and good times
> - *BACKBEAT RHYTHMS* — accents fall on beat 2 like in Motown, then on the final quaver of beat 4

Funk's More Rhythmic and Upbeat than Soul

Funk is kind of a dirtier, rougher version of soul.
Funk styles vary but blue notes, syncopation and distorted sounds are all common.

- The music's faster than soul. Rhythms are cut off and sound clipped.
- Bass guitar strings are slapped to give a popping, percussive sound.
- Rhythm guitar plays short rhythmic riffs using notes from the blues scale.
- Guitar and bass rhythms cut across one another, creating polyrhythms.
- The horns play riffs and full chords like in soul, but the riffs are faster and shorter.

Rock

The whole rock thing started in the <u>late 1960s</u> and it's been around ever since.

Guitars are a Big Deal in Heavy Rock

Heavy rock is the kind of thing played by <u>Led Zeppelin</u> and <u>Black Sabbath</u> (the band Ozzy Osbourne was in). Songs are built around <u>blues-style</u> guitar riffs and <u>blues scales</u>.

The guitar parts dominate and <u>guitar solos</u> are a big deal. Listen out for massive, crashing <u>power chords</u> (just the 1st and the 5th notes of the chord). They're sometimes turned up to <u>full volume</u> to give screeching <u>feedback</u> effects. To give the guitars even more oomph, the guitar and bass often <u>double up</u> on the main riffs. Drum rhythms are often <u>thumping</u> and energetic. Vocals are often sung in a <u>wailing gospel style</u>.

Heavy Metal Sounds More, er, Metallic

Heavy metal's <u>even harder</u> and <u>more distorted</u> than hard rock. There are <u>more guitar solos</u> and melody is often less important than creating a heavy, distorted sound. <u>Iron Maiden</u> are a fairly classic heavy metal band. <u>Thrash metal</u>, which was played by bands like <u>Megadeth</u> and <u>Metallica</u>, was even harder and faster.

Glam Rock is Theatrical and Glitzy

Glam Rock's easier to listen to than heavy rock, with a more <u>rock'n'roll</u> feel and catchy <u>hooks</u> and <u>tunes</u>. Performers (like David Bowie, Kiss and Gary Glitter) dressed up in <u>spangly catsuits</u> and wore lots of make-up.

In Progressive Rock the Tracks are Really Long

1) Songs on progressive (prog) rock albums are <u>longer</u> and <u>more complicated</u> than standard rock tracks. <u>Half a record</u> might be used for one continuous track.

2) Prog rock's often <u>thematic</u>, repeating the same ideas in different pieces, like in orchestral music.

3) You hear a lot of strung-out instrumentals and electronic effects.

4) Don't even try and make sense of the lyrics — they're often <u>mythical</u> and <u>nonsensical</u>.

5) Prog rock bands include <u>Yes</u>, <u>Genesis</u> and <u>Pink Floyd</u>.

Punk Rock's All About Anarchy and Rebellion

1) Punk rock was a <u>1970s</u> thing. Punks were <u>disgusted with society</u> and wrote about it in their lyrics. It's <u>harsh</u>, <u>angry</u> music — lyrics are more often <u>shouted</u> than sung.

2) Punk music uses a <u>basic</u> line-up of guitars, bass and drums. Listen out for <u>distorted</u>, <u>crashing</u> guitar sounds and very simple, fast, <u>thrashing</u> drum beats.

3) Tunes are based on just a few <u>major scale notes</u>.

4) British punk bands include <u>The Sex Pistols</u>, <u>The Damned</u> and <u>The Clash</u>. <u>Blondie</u> were from New York.

5) American punk had a bit of a revival in the 1990s with bands like <u>Green Day</u> and <u>The Offspring</u>.

Rock Music has Lived On

Rock reinvents itself from time to time...

1) In the 1980s the big rock stars were <u>U2</u>, <u>Bruce Springsteen</u>, <u>Bryan Adams</u> and <u>Guns'n'Roses</u>.

2) In the 1990s <u>grunge</u> took soft 1980s rock and toughened it up. American bands like <u>Nirvana</u>, <u>Pearl Jam</u> and <u>Alice in Chains</u> released records with a harder edge, talking about <u>drugs</u> and <u>mental illness</u>.

3) The early 2000s saw the arrival of nu-rock and nu-metal — bands like <u>Korn</u>, <u>Incubus</u> and <u>Linkin Park</u> mixing good old-fashioned rock and metal with elements of <u>rap</u> and <u>hip hop</u>.

Would anyone prefer a rock cake...

When you're revising, don't get bogged down in the teeny tiny details of different rock styles — it's much more important to learn the differences between <u>rock and reggae</u>, or <u>rock and soul</u>. It's easier too.

Folk-Influenced Pop

Folk music's got a bit of a crusty/flaky reputation — and it's probably fair enough.
But combined with pop music it becomes slightly <u>less crusty</u>...

Folk Music was the Music Played by Everyday People

Folk music is sung and played by <u>everyday people</u> — not megastars. <u>Most parts of the</u>
<u>world</u> have their own traditional folk music, e.g. mining songs from Yorkshire, or shepherds'
songs from Mongolia. <u>Cowboy songs</u>, <u>sea shanties</u>, <u>worksongs</u>, <u>love ballads</u>, <u>Irish jigs</u> and
<u>reels</u> are all folk music too. People don't play folk music so much nowadays because they
tend to play <u>recorded music</u> instead, but in the old days they couldn't get enough.

1) Folk tunes tend to be quite <u>simple</u>. The notes move in <u>steps</u>.

2) <u>All</u> the notes in a folk tune belong to the key. They're often based on <u>modes</u> or <u>pentatonic scales</u>
   (see Core book, P.17), but major and minor scales are used too.

3) Accompaniments are <u>simple chord patterns</u> played on <u>acoustic</u> instruments.

4) Examples of <u>traditional folk songs</u> are 'Danny Boy', 'Cockles and Mussels' and 'Scarborough Fair'.

Some Bands Mix Pop and Folk

There are some pop bands and performers who <u>mix</u> traditional
folk music from their country with pop instruments and styles.

1) *THE CORRS* use <u>Irish folk instruments</u> like the fiddle, bodhrán (a drum)
   and tin whistle, and <u>Irish dance rhythms</u> in their music.

2) *THE CHIEFTANS* are another Irish band. They play the <u>uillean pipes</u> (the Irish version of
   bagpipes) alongside pop instruments.

3) *ENYA* sings in <u>Gaelic</u>, the traditional language of Ireland. She mixes <u>synthesised orchestral</u>
   <u>sounds</u> with <u>traditional chords</u> and <u>harmonies</u>.

4) *THE POGUES* fused Irish folk music with <u>punk</u>. This style has been described as <u>thrash folk</u>.

Some Performers Play in a Folk Style

Other performers write completely original material in the style of <u>traditional folk music</u>.

BOB DYLAN

1) In the 1960s Dylan's music was all <u>simple folk-style tunes</u> accompanied by <u>acoustic guitar</u>. He sang
   in a <u>nasal</u>, <u>country and western</u> style and played the <u>harmonica</u> — just like his hero, the famous
   American folk singer <u>Woodie Guthrie</u>.

2) Dylan's lyrics are often quite <u>political</u>, on the side of ordinary people. In the USA, at protests against
   the <u>Vietnam war</u> and in support of <u>equal rights</u> for black people, protestors often sang Dylan's songs.

3) Later Dylan played his music backed by <u>amplified rock instruments</u> — this is known as <u>folk rock</u>.

   SIMON AND GARFUNKEL
   Simon and Garfunkel were around in the 1960s and 1970s. Their songs have a really <u>folky sound</u>.
   They even had a hit with the <u>traditional folk song</u> 'Scarborough Fair'. In their own songs, Paul Simon
   mostly sings <u>simple melody lines</u> and Art Garfunkel adds <u>harmonies</u> and <u>countermelodies</u>.

There's nowt so queer as folk...

I saw The Pogues once at Brixton Academy. The moshing was so severe I thought my head had come off
and I really did lose a shoe. Shane McGowan didn't have any teeth — I think he lost them all fighting.
But nothing beats a Pogues song for rowdy late-night singing. <u>Absolutely nothing</u>.

Fusion

Nope — this isn't a page about nuclear physics, it's about what happens when music styles from different cultures are blended, or fused, together. You get some really interesting results.

African Music Fusing with European Made Loads of Styles

1) The blues was created when African and European music fused together in America and the Caribbean in the early years of the slave trade. Jazz, gospel, reggae and soul all grew out of blues.

2) These styles have been imitated and developed in Western pop for years. Many African elements are so much part of pop music that you probably take them for granted. If the examiners ask about the African features in pop (and they probably will), write about...

| complex cross rhythms | repetition | unison backing vocals | call and response |

More recently, some performers have fused western pop styles with African ideas for special projects...

For the album *Graceland* Paul Simon worked with the South African band Ladysmith Black Mambazo — the album fuses their South African style with Western rock. Ladysmith Black Mambazo went on to sing with other Western pop artists, such as Lighthouse Family and Des'ree. Have a listen to their album *Ladysmith Black Mambazo In Harmony*.

Yousso N'dour and Neneh Cherry had a hit called '*7 Seconds*' in 1994 — it's a fusion of West African music with rock.

Some Fusion Borrows from Latin American Music

Some pop styles use musical ideas from Latin America — that's countries like Argentina, Brazil, Cuba and Puerto Rico. To spot a Latin feel, listen for two key things:

1) Offbeat rhythms from dances like samba, tango and rumba. Many songs use these rhythms alongside or instead of standard rock beats.
2) Latin American instruments. Percussion instruments like maracas, congas, bongos, guiro, claves and cowbell are used to give pop songs a Latin feel. Spanish-sounding guitar bits are often used to add to the Latin feel too.

Ricky Martin, Gloria Estefan and Santana are all famous for fusing Latin styles with Western pop.

In the UK Indian Styles are Often Fused with Pop

Music ideas from the Indian subcontinent are used more and more in Western pop. Kula Shaker and Cornershop are two of the more famous bands to fuse Western and Indian styles. Listen out for:

1) Indian instruments like the sitar (a stringed instrument) and tabla (Indian drums).
2) Tunes based on raga scales — sets of notes (or modes) used in Indian Classical music. They sound very different from Western major and minor scales.
3) Indian rhythm patterns — repeated patterns of beats called talas. Indian drummers improvise faster rhythms over the top of the tala and speak out rhythm words called bols while they're playing.

Bhangra was originally a traditional style from North India and Pakistan. It's been combined with Western pop style to create a whole new sound. This typical bhangra rhythm's often combined with reggae, rap and rock: Listen to the CD *A Rough Guide to Bhangra* to get the feel.

DHA NA NA NA NA DHA DHA NA

No marks will be awarded for con-fusion...

Think of fusion as an American hamburger with Indian mango chutney, or a bacon butty with Caribbean hot pepper sauce. Mix the right two flavours together and you could get something really tasty.

Revision Summary

This Area of Study — Popular Song Since 1960 — wins the special John Humphrys award for sounding most like a Mastermind topic. There's no black chair, no bright lights and no scary music and you can have more than two minutes if you want, but you can't pass on any of these — you've got to keep on doing them until you can get every last nit-picking one of them right without looking back at the section.

1) Name and describe five different vocal techniques.

2) Name and describe four different electronic effects used to manipulate voices in pop.

3) What two jobs do the guitars do in a pop band?

4) Does a bass guitar: a) strum chords   or,   b) play a low-sounding tune?

5) Name and describe seven guitar effects.

6) What's the drummer's main job in a pop band?

7) Write down as many differences as you can between a digital synth and an analogue synth.

8) What's the most commonly used pop song structure?

9) Write a definition of:
   a) a verse   b) a middle 8   c) a coda   d) a chorus

10) Name and describe four pop song structures, *apart from* the one you named in your answer to 9).

11) Draw a box diagram to show the chord changes in a 12-bar blues.

12) Write out a walking bass line to fit a 12-bar blues in G.

13) Which notes of a major scale do you flatten to make a blues scale? Write out a blues scale in G.

14) Name five features of jazz that crop up in pop.

15) Which two main styles combined to form rock'n'roll?

16) Elvis is the KING of rock'n'roll. Name two other rock'n'roll stars.

17) When did the Beatles come onto the pop scene?

18) Name three musical styles which the Beatles combined in their music.

19) What are the three main activities in a musical?

20) What were the first musicals called?

21) Name two famous musical writing partnerships.

22) In musicals what's the difference between an action song and a solo character song?

23) What's a ballad?

24) What four things would you expect to hear in a ballad song by a boy/girl band?

25) Where does reggae come from?

26) What's the general feel of a reggae song? Explain how the music creates the feel.

27) What are the two main types of soul music? Describe them both.

28) What makes funk different from soul?

29) Describe: a) heavy metal   b) heavy rock   c) glam rock   d) punk rock   e) prog rock

30) How can you recognise a folk tune?

31) Name two bands that mix pop instruments with traditional folk instruments from their country.

32) How did Bob Dylan use the folk tradition?

33) What's folk rock?

34) How do you create a fusion style?

35) Name four features of African music that you can hear in most pop songs.

36) How can you tell if a song's got Latin influence?

37) Write out the basic bhangra rhythm.

Air Guitar

Air guitar is a relatively <u>new</u> musical style. It developed about 20 or so years ago, when <u>Mr Osbourne</u> was famous for biting <u>bats' heads</u> off rather than moaning about his <u>wife's dogs</u> on Sky TV.

Air Guitar uses the Same Techniques as Real Guitar

First things first. Playing air guitar is <u>exactly the same</u> as playing a <u>real guitar</u>. The only difference is there's <u>no guitar</u>. So, like any beginner (real) guitarist, you need to learn some <u>basic techniques</u>:

1) Learn how to <u>hold</u> your 'guitar'. Find one that matches your <u>size</u>, and practise holding it in the <u>right position</u>. <u>Always</u> practise this in front of a <u>mirror</u>.

2) Get the <u>stance</u> right. Your <u>feet</u> should be <u>at least 60 cm apart</u>*.
For general posture ideas, think caveman/woman.

   * *This is only true if you're playing rock music from the 70s onwards. For example, if you were playing 50s-style rock'n'roll you would need an entirely different stance — feet together, no movement from waist down, top half of body swaying from left to right, cheesy grin...*

3) Make sure you always look like you're <u>concentrating</u> *really really* hard.
This is particularly important during <u>widdly bits</u>.

4) <u>Hair</u> time. If you don't have <u>long hair</u>, it's very important that you pretend you do have <u>long hair</u>. Move the head forwards and backwards in time with the music, throwing your <u>hair</u> everywhere. If you're doing it properly you should soon notice your <u>hair</u> starting to stick to your sweaty face and get caught in your mouth and nose. Perfect this <u>hair</u> technique and you're well on your way.

(60 cm)

You need to Learn the Three Classic Moves:

The 'Down-on-One-Knee' Manoeuvre is Easy

head leaning back in concentration

right <u>knee</u> on <u>floor</u>

air guitar held proudly <u>aloft</u>

'The Windmill' Takes a Bit More Practice...

right hand forming <u>perfect circles</u>

The <u>trick</u> is getting the circle to pass through the point where you would hit the strings (if you were playing a <u>real</u> guitar). This requires both <u>technique</u> and <u>confidence</u>. It's easy to look like a <u>nonce</u> if you mess it up.

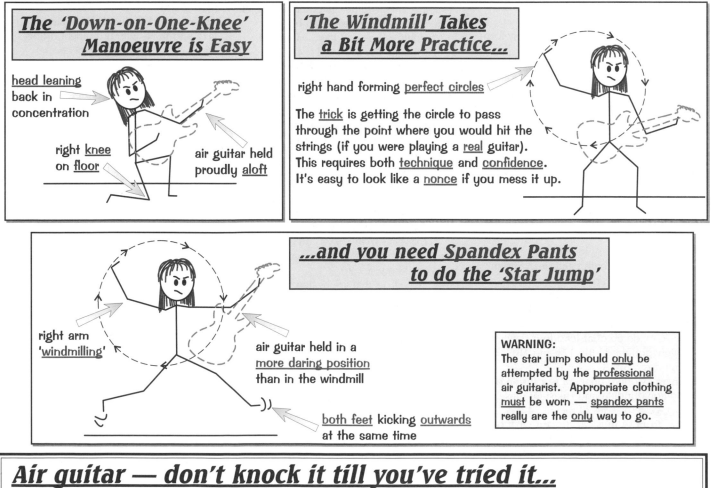

...and you need Spandex Pants to do the 'Star Jump'

right arm '<u>windmilling</u>'

air guitar held in a <u>more daring position</u> than in the windmill

<u>both feet</u> kicking <u>outwards</u> at the same time

WARNING:
The star jump should <u>only</u> be attempted by the <u>professional</u> air guitarist. Appropriate clothing <u>must</u> be worn — <u>spandex pants</u> really are the <u>only</u> way to go.

Air guitar — don't knock it till you've tried it...

And finally... I'd like to finish off the page with a list of recommended tunes to practise air guitar to.
1. Sweet Child of Mine (G'n'R)   2. Eye of the Tiger (Survivor)   3. Bohemian Rhapsody (Queen)
4. Run to the Hills (Iron Maiden)   5. Livin' on a Prayer (Bon Jovi)   6. Money for Nothing (Dire Straits)

Glossary and Index

As I'm sure you're all-too-painfully aware, there's a staggering number of technical terms that you're expected to learn for GCSE Music. So I thought a bit of a glossary-type-thing wouldn't go amiss here...

A

a cappella Singing with no instrumental backing. The term comes from the Italian for 'in the chapel'. **37**

agitato In an agitated style. **33**

aleatoric Music that is composed or performed with an intentional element of chance. This is a style of **twentieth century orchestral music**. **35**

ambient Tranquil and ethereal **club dance music**. **19**

amoroso In a loving style. This often appears in **Romantic** music. **33**

anacrusis An unstressed note or group of notes at the start of a phrase, before the strong first beat of the bar. **14, 26**

appoggiatura One of the notes in a chord can be split into two notes — the note itself and the one just above or below it (the **appoggiatura**). The appoggiatura's played first and clashes with the rest of the chord, then the note in the chord is played (the resolution). **16**

aria An elaborate song for solo voice in **opera**. **24**

arpeggio The notes of a chord played in succession, either going up or down. **32**

Atlantic soul A rough-edged, bluesy form of **soul** music. **44**

atonality Using notes that aren't from any particular **key**. Commonly used in **twentieth century orchestral music**. **35**

B

backbeat rhythms Accents fall on the second beat of the bar and the final quaver of beat 4. **44**

ballad A song that tells a story. In pop and rock music, ballads tend to tell love stories. **43**

Baroque Musical style of the seventeenth and early eighteenth centuries. Strong bass and lots of ornamentation. J.S. Bach and Handel were two of the greatest Baroque composers. **14-15**

Baroque suite A piece of instrumental music made up of at least four dances, hugely popular in the 17th and 18th centuries. **14-15**

bhangra Modern bhangra is a **fusion** of traditional Indian and Pakistani music with western styles of music. **47**

binary form A musical structure that has two distinct sections. **15, 17**

blues Afro-American folksong, usually sad and slow. See also **blues notes** and **12-bar blues**. **40**

blues notes The flattened 3rd and 7th and sometimes 5th notes that appear in the major key in **blues** music, giving it the distinctive blues feel. **40**

boogie-woogie bass Type of **walking bass** played in a dotted rhythm. Used in **jazz**, **rhythm'n'blues** and **pop**. **40**

brass Family of wind instruments including trumpet, trombone, tuba and French horn. **17, 32, 44**

C

cadence The movement from the second-to-last chord to the last chord in a phrase. They make the end of the phrase feel like an ending. **15, 30**

cadenza A flourish near the end of a **concerto** or **aria** in which the soloist shows off his or her virtuosity. It was originally improvised, but many composers have since written out what they want the soloist to play. **30**

call A short **melody**, followed by a **response**, that together gives the feeling of a 'question and answer'. Can be on instruments or voice. Often features in **12-bar blues**. **29, 37, 39, 41, 44**

canon Piece of music which relies on the imitation of one **theme**. **8**

chromatics Notes that don't belong to the main **key** of a melody. **11, 16, 32, 33, 41**

Classical <u>Either</u> any music that's not **pop** (or **jazz**, **folk**, **R&B**, etc.) <u>or</u> music composed in Europe in the late 18th and early 19th centuries. Two of the greatest Classical composers were Haydn and Mozart. **28-31**

     Classical period **28-31, 36**
     Classical orchestra **28-31, 36**
     Classical style **29-31, 36**

clave A basic repeated rhythm pattern, the basis of **son** music. **20**

claves Two sticks that are beaten together to give the **clave** rhythm. **20**

club dance music Varieties of club dance include **techno**, **jungle**, **trance** and **drum'n'bass**. **18-19**

coda The ending to a piece of music. (It means 'tail' in Italian.) **39**

comping Playing rhythmic chords on the piano or guitar to accompany the tune. It is a feature of **salsa** and **jazz**. **21**

composition **2-3**

composition brief **2**

concerto Piece of music written for one solo instrument and an orchestra. It is usually written in three movements. **30**

coursework **1-5**

crescendo Gradual increase in volume. **7**

D

descant A harmonising tune sung at the same time as the main melody but higher. **37**

diegetic music When the characters in a film can actually hear the music. **8, 9**

digital effects Special effects used in **club dance**, such as **reverb** and **vocoder**. **19**

diminished chord When the 5th of the chord is lowered by a semi-tone. This creates an unsettling sound, often to be heard in classic **horror** films. **10**

diminuendo Gradual decrease in volume. **7**

disco Dance music that originated in nightclubs in the 1970s, characterised by a simple beat and catchy tunes. **18**

dolce Sweetly (an instruction to performers). **33**

drum'n'bass A **fusion** of **club dance**, **jazz** and **funk**, with prominent drums and bass (as you might expect). **19**

duple metre Metre used in dance, with 2 beats per bar. **13**

dynamics Variations in loudness which affect the **mood** of the piece. **7, 10, 33**

E

~~**Eye of the Tiger**~~ Song by Survivor that's a favourite with any self-respecting air guitarist **49**

F

falsetto When a male singer sings notes higher than his normal range. Often used in **Baroque** and **pop** music. **37**

fanfare Tune played on **brass** and percussion instruments using the notes of simple chords. Played at important formal events. **24**

fantasy (The film genre, not the lustful thought.) **10**

film music **7-11**

folk music Traditional music played by the ordinary people of a country or region. **46**

folk dance Traditional dances performed at public events, such as Morris dancing and maypole dancing. **13**

Glossary and Index

Glossary and Index